COOKING

OFF THE CLOCK

COOKING
OFF THE CLOCK

RECIPES FROM MY DOWNTIME

Elizabeth Falkner

photography by Frankie Frankeny

TEN SPEED PRESS
Berkeley

Contents

Introduction

I COOK PROFESSIONALLY, for the rush and for fun, and I cook to relax and take care of myself. When I come home after working at the restaurants all day and night, I am hungry and have the energy for more. That may sound strange because I am surrounded by food all the time, but it's true. I love cooking in competition also, which is a sort of ultimate test of cooking in a specific time frame and pulling out the best cook and performer I can be under the lights, camera, and pressure.

People always think that while you are cooking, you must be eating, but that's not what really happens. As a chef, I constantly taste while I am cooking at work and when I come home I am needing balance and am hungry for dinner, playtime, and downtime. Cooking and entertaining is how I enjoy making people happy, as well as nurturing them when they are at the table at the restaurant or at a dinner party. I want the same kind of satisfaction at the end of a day or on an off day. Also, running around the restaurant all night is a serious body-warping workout that can be physically and mentally exhausting. I have my dogs to come home to and I work out a lot, mixing it up with yoga, kickboxing, boxing, and Korean swordfighting. My days and nights are in constant motion so, when I get home or have a day off to cook for my friends, I'm ready to eat. And, believe it or not, I'm excited to cook, too.

Cooking all day and working with my crews and cooking at events are fun and it's my job, but when I cook at home, it is usually about relaxing and preparing something without the pressures in the restaurants. I make things that don't take much time or effort, and if I am craving something that does take a little more time, such as Beef Stroganoff (page 144) I will start preparing it while I cook something else that I am definitely going to eat sooner, such as Grilled Pork Chop (page 139).

You'll recognize some of these recipes as classics, but with unexpected nuances or twists, because analyzing and reinventing a dish is exactly what I do as a chef.

Often I come home from work and despite my good intentions, I really don't have much in the way of fabulous ingredients on hand. I might have a few cans of things and a stash of good spices and luckily a few pots of cooking herbs on the patio. Here's where I must rely on my creativity and palate to come up with something satisfying and delicious. I find this an exercise in humility to let the ingredients speak for themselves, and I just have to pay attention. Sometimes these are the best recipes, and I have included many of them in this book.

The first chapter of this book offers recipes for my favorite condiments, including a great steak sauce, an endlessly useful tomato sauce, and a creamy horseradish sauce to wake up meat, plus basics like simple chicken and beef stocks, crunchy bread crumbs, and the best ways to cook eggs—coddled to hard-boiled to deviled. All are great additions that add layers of flavors to the recipes throughout the book. For most of these condiments, though, if making your own just seems like too much work, you can substitute store-bought. For example, you just cannot deal with making stock, buy cartons of chicken, beef, or vegetable broth.

In this book, I'll show you how to stock your pantry, plan a little for more efficient cooking, shop for great ingredients and be inspired by them, think about combinations, and prepare delicious dishes. When I go to the market for myself, I try to think about what I am craving that week. I might buy whatever produce looks good at the time, pick out some meat or poultry and keep them in the freezer, and grab a few basic pantry ingredients, like garlic, potatoes, herbs, cheese, canned tomatoes, ginger, olives, and things that if you have on hand, just make it easier to come home and whip something up. I have written most of the recipes to serve two to four. However, I am often just cooking for myself or maybe another person or two, so cutting the recipe in half or in quarters should be easy to do here as well as doubling it to serve six to eight.

Typically, I go through phases when I get obsessed about reinterpreting a classic dish in a new and great way, or using as many tomatoes as possible at their seasonal peak. Or it's an obsession with a regional cuisine or a technique I really want to master. This usually spills into making it both at work and at home. This sort of challenge is almost a game for me, in a way, because it's how I keep food ideas coming. My home kitchen becomes my laboratory. From there, I might interpret those ideas for the restaurants.

THE PANTRY: HOW TO STOCK IT

I often shop at farmers' markets, mostly for the restaurants, but once in a while for myself. The freshness, variety, and quality of what I find there, particularly produce picked in season and just hours from the farm, is unbeatable. For my home pantry, I shop at a supermarket and some specialty shops—the sources for most of the ingredients in this book.

□ Oils

I do like to have a basic inexpensive olive oil for starting sautés and for general cooking. Canola oil is great for frying and for mayonnaise. And a flavorful, extra-virgin olive oil for vinaigrettes and for finishing dishes.

□ Spices

Spices are a pantry necessity. I prefer buying them as whole seeds—particularly nutmeg, fennel, cumin, and coriander seed—that I toast, grind, or grate, as they add considerably more flavor to a dish than the powdered forms. You can use preground spices to substitute for whole ones here, but make sure the powered spice is fresh and has aroma before adding it to anything. If it smells like dust, it will taste like dust. The problem is that as soon as spices are ground, the volatile oils, which equal flavor, get released in the air, so it is best to grind a spice just before adding it to a dish.

□ Chiles and Chile Powders

I am crazy for all kinds of chiles, and I stock *piment d'Espelette*—the Basque chile—when I can find it, as well as ancho and chipotle chiles. Other forms include cayenne pepper; pimentón, the sweet and spicy Spanish smoked paprika, pure ground chile powders, and red pepper flakes. I do not use the preground chile spice blend that is labled "chili" on supermarket spice shelves.

□ Other Spices and Herbs

Star anise is a spice that first of all is beautiful and looks like a little pinwheel. It has a flavor like root beer and licorice and is a wonderful aromatic in Asian dishes such as pho or in marinades and sauces. Whole nutmegs are easy to use and grate into sauces, desserts, and even hot chocolate. I keep fenugreek, allspice, cinnamon sticks, whole cloves, and dried oregano in my spice drawer. As for herbs, I mostly use fresh herbs and not dried. With all of these in my pantry, I can conjure up something to eat and feel like I have traveled somewhere exotic.

I am a black pepper fan and am not sold on pink peppercorn or green or even white pepper or a blend of them. I use black peppercorns in a pepper grinder and never preground pepper. I use two salts primarily. I use kosher salt in just about everything from seasoning meat to vinaigrettes and baking. Once in a while I add a little *fleur de sel* (sea salt) to finish a dish and get that extra crunch of salt on tomatoes or avocados or on a grilled steak.

◻ Other Pantry Items

I usually keep some canned tomatoes, dried chickpeas, Dijon and whole-grain mustards, cornichons (still my favorite pickle of baby cucumbers), and *harissa*—a North African spicy chile paste condiment. I also keep handy a few kinds of dried pasta or noodles as well as rice. Also on hand are chunks of Parmesan cheese and/or pecorino, to grate, not pregrated, Asian fish sauce, ketchup, and a few vinegars, such as champagne, white wine, sherry, red wine, and aged balsamic.

PASTRY PANTRY

Of course, as a pastry chef, I do consider brown sugar, large eggs (the default size for all the recipes in this cookbook), unsalted butter, all-purpose flour, bittersweet chocolate, and cocoa powder as staples.

IN THE FREEZER

I recommend keeping some bacon and/or pancetta in the freezer because everything really does improve with the addition of cured pork. I also make chicken stock once in a while at home and keep portions of it in containers in the freezer. Good ice is essential for great cocktails, so keep some clean ice in the freezer, meaning it has not been sitting in the freezer for more than a month and picked up other flavors and freezer burn.

USEFUL EQUIPMENT AND TOOLS

As a chef, I am always interested in new equipment and kitchen toys to experiment with, but at home I turn to the basics. The ones I have listed here I find especially helpful.

I recommend whisks for vinaigrette; a few decent sharp knives such as a 10-inch chef's knife, a serrated knife, and a small paring knife; plus a cutting board to use them on. I have a large wooden cutting board as well as a couple of small bamboo ones that I use most often. In addition, I find the following items indispensible.

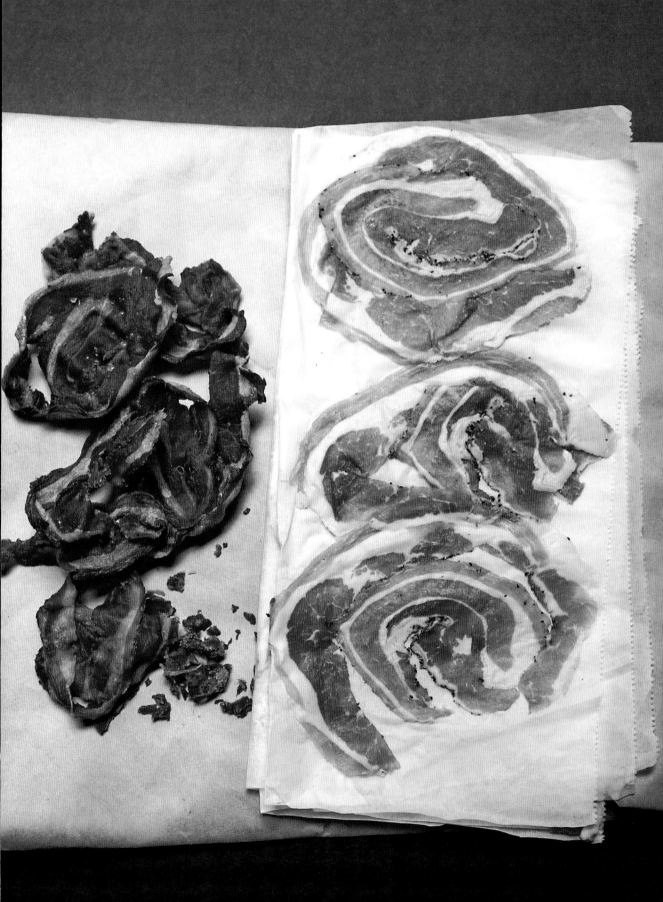

□ Mandoline

I use a small and inexpensive Japanese-made mandoline to shave vegetables thin.

□ Heavy-Duty Stand Mixer

I prefer using my hands for just about everything when cooking at home, but a heavy-duty stand mixer is particularly helpful with making doughs or whipping up egg whites.

□ Blender

I use a bar blender for pureeing soups and sauces at home

□ Food Processor

I use a food processor for making mayonnaise and for some quick grinding of nuts and bread crumbs.

□ Pastry Bag and Tips

I use the cloth pastry bags and simple star tip or tube tip for easy decorative piping for whipped cream, frosting, and the yolk filling in deviled eggs.

□ Barbecue Grill

Like a lot of Americans, I like to grill outdoors. I have a propane-fueled grill on the patio and actually find it easy to cook with at any time. My neighbors probably think I have strange midnight snack attacks, but I'm just cooking a late dinner.

□ Cast-Iron Skillet

I have a few of these pans that have been passed down to me from my mother and my grandmother. I use a smaller one all the time for quick toasting of spices and nuts and recommend using a large one for making griddled pizza. Cooking a strip steak on the extra high heat in a cast-iron pan gives the meat a superior caramelized crust. An extra bonus of cooking with cast iron is that it actually adds iron to a dish, and we need extra iron in our diets.

□ Heavy-Gauge Cookware

Seriously, you need to have heavy-gauge cookware to get great results in cooking. The thin stuff isn't going to cut it because the heat is inconsistent in the less expensive cookware. You only need a saucepan, a large sauté pan and a medium stockpot for most everything. A small sauté pan and a large stockpot are helpful in addition. I look for stainless steel lined aluminum core or enamel lined cookware.

□ Immersion Blender

It is just so easy to use an immersion blender, which is a handheld wand with the blender attachment at the end that you simply stick into a pot or container to puree sauces.

□ Microwave Oven

A microwave oven can be a timesaver for an initial steaming of potatoes before finishing in a hot oven, and for quick defrosting and melting chocolate.

□ Mortar and Pestle

I use this traditional tool, which consists of a bowl-shaped container and a handheld pounder of the same material—usually marble, ceramic, or wood—for grinding spices and crushing nuts. An electric spice grinder is fine, too.

□ Pepper Mill and Ramekins for Salt

I recommend always using freshly ground pepper instead of the ground pepper from a tin. I have a couple of pepper mills, because in addition to being useful, they are decorative. I have a couple of pewter ones made by Peugot and I have a tall wooden one.

I keep two little bowls of salt right by my stove. One is filled with kosher salt that I use for everything and the other with *fleur de sel*, the French sea salt that I use to finish dishes.

□ Vegetable Peeler

I use a vegetable peeler mostly for making shavings from a wedge of Parmesan or ricotta salata cheese, and for shaving carrots and summer squash into thin ribbons, as well as for peeling potatoes or orange peel for a negroni.

□ Microplane Grater

The Microplane grater is probably the most handy tool in the professional and home kitchen today. It is smaller and handier compared to the classic box graters, and the grate size is smaller, so it is great for grating zest and thin shreds of cheese. I use Microplane rasp-style graters for creating thin shreds of fresh horseradish and grating zest from lemons or other citrus.

□ Wire-Mesh Colander or Simple 6-inch Wire Strainer

I seem to use both of these all the time for rinsing off lettuces and other produce, straining pasta, and for sifting. I have a medium-size wire-mesh colander and a medium-size strainer with a handle as well as a small cup-size strainer. None of them is super-fine mesh, like a Chinoise, which we use more often in a professional kitchen.

CONDIMENTS AND BASICS

MAKING YOUR OWN condiments or basics like stocks may seem like you're investing more time than you may have. But homemade mayonnaise or steak sauce or kimchee offers delicious rewards: mayonnaise can be turned into a peanut emulsion for the Chinese Chicken Salad (page 50), curry mayonnaise for fries or a sandwich, or tartar sauce for fish and chips. And when I make steaks for a party with homemade steak sauce on the side or pork chops with homemade kimchee, everyone feels I have gone above and beyond their expectations.

Sometimes the task isn't as complicated as it appears, although store-bought staples like mayonnaise, stocks, and pastas are perfectly okay to use. Do a little comparison shopping to get to know which brands you prefer so it's easy to grab your favorites during an after-work, market fly-by if that's how you want to go that day. And, if you have a little time to make them from scratch, great. Some of these recipes are my quick tricks, some are my favorite condiments, and all are foundation tools for great food.

EGGS: AS I LIKE THEM

Whenever I cook eggs, Hudson, a Yorkshire terrier, and Hendrix, a dachshund, never take their eyes off of me. As soon as they hear the cracking of an eggshell, they watch with full attention, just in case I decide to make a little bite for each of them, which I do every once in a while and serve in small soy sauce dishes. (They are both small dogs and neither needs a big bowl of any food.) They love eggs as much as I do.

I cook and eat eggs in many different forms. I find that I enjoy them medium-boiled and then cut into halves or quarters, as in Tomato-Centric Cobb Salad (page 36). Or, just the yolks cooked with a little pasta water, as I do for Carbonara (page 125). Or, a classic poached egg simply paired with toast or the Shaved Summer Squash salad (page 40). For a late Sunday breakfast or as an anytime snack, I do crave perfectly scrambled eggs with grilled asparagus and crostini—that addictive Italian toast.

Choose eggs that are from free-roaming or free-range birds, because the birds have had less stress and better diets, and I like supporting farmers who tend to animals this way rather than exploiting the chickens with little real estate, no movement, and a tremendous amount of stress and anxiety. I don't want to eat an animal or its eggs that is not treated humanely. Buy them as fresh as possible—the fresher they are, the better they'll taste. And fresh eggs are better to cook with. Every technique we use with eggs works best when the eggs are fresh. You'll often find a good selection from local sources at farmers' markets.

I feel that one must learn how to cook eggs as a foundation for a better understanding of cooking. Following are instructions for cooking eggs in what I think are the most useful, versatile ways. I use large eggs, so you may need to adjust cooking times if using smaller or larger eggs.

Coddled EGGS

I coddle eggs in the shell to kill any possible salmonella. I do this for any recipe that calls for a raw egg or raw egg yolk. I would use a coddled egg in a Caesar dressing or for mayonnaise. This technique doesn't cook the egg completely, but makes using raw eggs safe.

○ Use large eggs that are at room temperature. Fill a saucepan with enough water to cover the eggs by 1 inch and bring to a boil over high heat. Carefully lower the eggs into the water and turn off the heat. Let the eggs sit in the water for 1 minute (2 minutes if coddling eggs directly from the refrigerator) and then rinse them under cold running water to stop the cooking.

Soft-Boiled EGGS

○ Use large eggs that are at room temperature. Fill a saucepan with enough water to cover the eggs by 1 inch and bring to a boil over high heat. Carefully lower the eggs into the water, decrease the heat to a simmer, and cook for 4 to 5 minutes. Have an ice bath (a bowl of ice water) ready. Transfer the eggs to the ice bath for 30 seconds to stop the cooking. The egg whites will be set, and the yolks will be thickened liquid.

Medium-Boiled EGGS

○ I prefer medium-boiled eggs for the Tomato-Centric Cobb Salad (page 36). Follow the directions for preparing soft-boiled eggs, but cook for 6 to 7 minutes.

Hard-Boiled EGGS

○ I use hard-boiled eggs for Deviled Eggs (page 15) and for shaving over salads or in the Cobb Relish (page 18). Follow the directions for preparing soft-boiled eggs, but cook for 9 to 10 minutes.

Remove the soft- to hard-boiled eggs from the ice bath after about 30 seconds. Gently roll the egg on the counter so the shell is crackled all over. Drop the egg back into the ice bath. The water will slip between the shell and the white, making it easier to remove the shell. Rinse the peeled egg under cool running water and use as desired.

I rarely store any precooked eggs and believe they are just tastier if used right away. If you do hard-boil some eggs before you need them, keep them in their shells in the refrigerator.

Poached EGGS

Poached eggs are great simply with toast, or with eggs Benedict, pasta, or the classic French-style frisée salad with lardons with a shallot vinaigrette.

○ For 1 to 4 large eggs, fill a wide saucepan about half full of water and bring it to a boil. Add 2 teaspoons salt and 1 teaspoon white wine vinegar. For each egg, crack onto a flat surface (like a plate) and gently slide the egg into the water. Decrease the heat to a low simmer. With a small strainer or a spoon, skim off any part of the egg white that separates on the surface. Let the eggs poach until the whites are set but the yolks are still runny, about 5 minutes (or more if you like a firmer yolk). Remove with a slotted spoon and drain off any excess water by holding the spoon over a clean kitchen towel or a paper towel. Use as desired.

Note: For large parties, you can poach the eggs in advance. Poach for 5 minutes, carefully slide them into an ice bath (a bowl of ice water) to stop the cooking, remove with a slotted spoon into a pan, and reserve in the refrigerator until it's time to serve them. Then slip them back into just simmered hot water for 30 seconds to warm them up.

Condiments and Basics

Scrambled EGGS

I cannot scramble just one egg. It is too small of an amount and too easy to overcook, so I recommend scrambling at least two eggs per person. You can cook the eggs in butter, olive oil, or chicken, duck, or bacon fat. All are great and each transforms the flavor of the eggs in a unique way. You can buy duck fat, and you can also make duck or chicken fat by cooking the skin in a saucepan over low heat until all of the fat has rendered out, 10 to 20 minutes. It is the same when you cook bacon. Simply reserve the fat and keep covered in the freezer for later use.

MAKES 1 SERVING

2 large eggs

1 tablespoon heavy cream or whole milk

1 tablespoon unsalted butter; or chicken, duck, or bacon fat; or olive oil

Salt and freshly ground black pepper

○ Crack the eggs into a bowl and whisk in the cream.

○ Heat a skillet over medium-high heat and add the butter, fat, or oil. Add the eggs and decrease the heat to low. After about 1 minute, with a wooden spoon or rubber spatula, pull the eggs from the outside toward the inside where they are cooking fastest. Cook for another 15 seconds and repeat. Season with salt and pepper. Flip the mixture around for another 15 to 20 seconds.

○ Remove from the heat and serve immediately. They will continue to cook even after you have removed them from the pan.

Deviled EGGS

Happily, deviled eggs—that fixture at bridge luncheons and bridal showers of the 1940s and '50s—are back, and why not? They are a perfect hors d'oeuvre, tasty and easy to eat, as well as a satisfying snack, day or night. Here's my basic recipe, elevated with a little crème fraîche, plus suggestions for simple ways to reinvent this very versatile finger food (see Flavor and Finishing Options, following). Deviled eggs can be made a few hours in advance and kept covered in the refrigerator; however, a bit of a skin will form on the yolk mixture, so I prefer to make the yolk mixture and pipe or set it in the whites just before serving.

MAKES 8 DEVILED EGGS

4 large Hard-Boiled Eggs, peeled (page 12),

1 teaspoon Dijon mustard

2 tablespoons crème fraîche

1 tablespoon olive oil

$^1/_4$ teaspoon salt

Freshly ground black pepper

Freshly squeezed lemon juice

○ Carefully halve each egg across its midsection into 2 equal pieces. Scoop out the yolks and mash with a fork in a bowl. Mix in the mustard, crème fraîche, olive oil, salt, pepper, and lemon juice. Taste for seasoning. If adding any other ingredients to the yolk mixture (see Flavor and Finishing Options, following), add them now.

○ Spoon the yolk mixture into a pastry bag with a plain or star tip and pipe into the cavity of each egg white. Or place a mound of the mixture into the cavity of each egg white with a spoon. Keep covered in the refrigerator if not eating or serving immediately. Garnish with any of the options for finishes, if desired.

Flavor and Finishing Options

For additional flavor, stir in any of the following to the yolk mixture: 1 teaspoon minced fresh tarragon, a pinch of pimentón (Spanish smoked paprika) or cayenne pepper, a few fine gratings of lemon zest, or $^1/_2$ teaspoon truffle oil.

To finish, garnish the yolk mixture with any of the following: a few grains of sea salt— either *fleur de sel* or Maldon; 2 or 3 capers, minced fresh parsley, a sliver of anchovy with or without a sliver of roasted piquillo pepper, or shaved fresh truffle.

Habanero BBQ SYRUP

I call this a syrup rather than a sauce because it is not as thick as the typical BBQ sauce. The uber-heat of roasted habanero chile achieves balance from the bitter sweetness of the molasses and *ketjap manis* (an Indonesian sweet soy sauce). Apple cider vinegar and tamarind add a contrasting acidity. I pair this with fried chicken and use it as a great alternative sauce for chicken wings (page 75). Try it, too, as a baste for meat loaf or even grilled chicken. Tamarind is a pod or legume that grows in the Equatorial belt. It looks like a brown skinned large pea or fava pod and has hard seeds and a thick pasty fruit that has a good amount of acidity. Tamarind concentrate can be found in Latin and Asian markets as well as Whole Foods Markets.

MAKES ABOUT 2 CUPS

1 habanero chile, char-grilled or broiled until blackened and sweated

1/2 cup plus 2 tablespoons molasses

5 tablespoons ketjap manis

1/4 cup plus 1 tablespoon apple cider vinegar

3/4 teaspoon garlic powder

2 teaspoons tamarind concentrate

1/4 cup honey

2 tablespoons Dijon mustard

1/2 cup plus 1 tablespoon ketchup

○ Wearing gloves to protect your hands from the chile's volatile oils, remove most of the charred skin and all the seeds from the habanero. In a small saucepan, combine the chile, molasses, *ketjap manis*, vinegar, garlic, tamarind, and honey and bring just to a boil over high heat.

○ Remove from the heat and let cool slightly. Add the Dijon mustard and ketchup to the syrup and pour into a blender and puree or use an immersion blender to puree right in the pan.

○ Stored in an airtight container, the syrup will last up to 2 months in the refrigerator.

Brown Butter BÉARNAISE

Let's be realistic: béarnaise—one of the classic French sauces—is not for beginning cooks. It's not complicated to make, it's just that the ingredients have to emulsify at close to the same temperature, and slowly, and when they don't, the sauce looks like a total disaster. It dawned on me several years ago that pretty much every recipe that emphasizes butter is that much better when the butter is browned, because the sugars in the milk solids caramelize, and we all like caramelized flavors. I started making steaks at home with brown butter béarnaise and when I opened Orson restaurant, one of the dishes I wanted to serve was duck-fat-fried French fries served with brown butter béarnaise. Just by browning the butter, the recipe is transformed into a classic sauce with a lot more flavor. It was an immediate hit.

MAKES ABOUT 1 CUP

$^3/_4$ cup ($1^1/_2$ sticks) unsalted butter, cut into small chunks

$^1/_2$ cup white wine vinegar

1 shallot with peel left on, halved

6 whole black peppercorns

1 sprig tarragon

4 large egg yolks

Pinch of sugar

$^1/_4$ cup canola oil

2 tablespoons freshly squeezed lemon juice

$1^1/_2$ teaspoons salt

1 tablespoon chopped fresh tarragon

○ To brown the butter, set a heatproof container in an ice bath (a bowl of ice water) and have ready. Put the chunks of butter in a small saucepan over low heat. The butter will melt, foam, and start to caramelize and turn brown (which will make the whole house smell wonderful and nutty) in about 8 to10 minutes. As soon as it hits this fragrance and color, remove the pan from the heat and pour into the heatproof container in the ice bath to stop the cooking; otherwise, that fantastic fragrance will quickly turn into a burned nasty fragrance. Set aside to cool. When completely cool, the butter will set up as a solid again, but can be made liquid again on the stove or in the microwave to use in the rest of the recipe.

○ In a small saucepan, combine the white wine vinegar, shallot, peppercorns, and tarragon over medium-low heat; cook until reduced by half the volume. Set aside to cool.

○ Bring a saucepan filled halfway with water to a gentle simmer. In a large heatproof bowl, whisk the egg yolks and sugar until combined. Strain the cooled reduced vinegar mixture into the bowl and whisk well. Discard the shallots and peppercorns. Put the bowl over the simmering water. Whisk constantly until the egg mixture is thick and foamy, like a sabayon or foamed egg dessert. This will only take a couple of minutes. You want to whip air into the mixture and gently cook the egg yolks. The mixture will be warm to the touch and will

(continued)

begin to hold the trail of the whisk, 2 to 3 minutes. Immediately remove from the heat and continue whisking for another 30 seconds. Do not stop whisking or the eggs can overcook.

○ Pour the mixture into a blender. With the motor running, slowly add the canola oil and then the lemon juice. Warm the cooled brown butter in the microwave or on the stove just to melt it and be slightly warm but not hot. Now add the brown butter slowly with the salt, and puree for 1 minute. If the mixture is too thick to pour, add hot water to the running blender a tablespoon at a time until the desired consistency is reached. Transfer the béarnaise to a bowl and stir in the chopped tarragon.

○ Use immediately or set the bowl over warm (not simmering or boiling) water, stirring occasionally, until ready to use. I have found that I can cover and chill the sauce and bring to room temperature at a later date and puree again to use.

COBB RELISH

I use this zesty relish on burgers, to garnish tomatoes for a quick salad, with fried chicken, or as a spread on a roast beef sandwich. My inspiration—a burger, of course! I wanted to partner the burger with bacon, blue cheese, and egg, but without the mess of stacking one on the other.

MAKES ABOUT 1 CUP

1 slice bacon

2 large Hard-Boiled Eggs (page 12), finely chopped

2 tablespoons finely crumbled blue cheese (about 1 ounce), such as Maytag or Point Reyes Blue

1 tablespoon minced fresh Italian parsley

1/4 teaspoon finely grated lemon zest

Salt and freshly ground black pepper

○ Cook the bacon in a small sauté pan until rendered and crisp. Drain on a clean kitchen towel or paper towel. Let cool completely and finely chop. In a bowl, combine the chopped bacon, eggs, blue cheese, parsley, lemon zest, salt, and pepper, and toss gently together. I prefer not to refrigerate this mixture and instead use it all immediately.

HARISSA

From the fiery cuisines of North Africa comes this hot condiment that is used like a salsa. It is a favorite with lamb but also enhances fish, chicken, and grilled or raw vegetables. There are many versions, but it typically consists of chiles, garlic, cumin, cayenne, and other spices, plus olive oil. This one has some fire and the surprise of one of my all-time favorite ingredients—rose water. It's rather concentrated, so just a tablespoon or two can add pizzazz to a vinaigrette or a dip made with chickpea puree or yogurt. Typically found in Middle Eastern markets, rose water is carried in most markets these days. Similarly, pimentón (smoked paprika) from Spain is widely available and comes in mild, medium, and hot options. I usually use the medium, or "agro-dulce."

MAKES ABOUT 2 CUPS

4 dried ancho chiles, stemmed and seeded

1 medium roasted red bell pepper, or 4 ounces piquillo peppers

2 cloves garlic

1 tablespoon sherry vinegar

1 tablespoon freshly squeezed lemon juice

3 tablespoons tomato paste

$1/4$ teaspoon cumin seeds, toasted and ground

$1/4$ teaspoon cayenne pepper

$1/4$ teaspoon pimentón (Spanish smoked paprika)

$1/2$ teaspoon rose water

$3/4$ cup olive oil

2 teaspoons salt

○ Cover the chiles with boiling water and let sit uncovered to rehydrate for 5 to 10 minutes. Drain and put in a blender with the bell pepper, garlic, vinegar, lemon juice, tomato paste, cumin, cayenne, pimentón, and rose water. Puree, then slowly add the olive oil. Adjust the seasoning with salt. Store in an airtight container in the refrigerator for up to 2 months.

Condiments and Basics

HORSERADISH Cream

This is a great accompaniment to any beef dish, such as the carpaccio with roasted beet salad (page 47), but is also great with a grilled steak, beef short ribs, or on baked potatoes.

MAKES ¹/₂ CUP

¹/₂ cup crème fraîche

1 tablespoon grated fresh horseradish, or
  1 teaspoon prepared horseradish

Freshly ground black pepper

○ In a small bowl, whisk the crème fraîche until slightly thickened. Stir in the horseradish and pepper. Stored in an airtight container, it will keep for 1 week in the refrigerator.

KIMCHEE

I love the often incendiary Korean pickled-vegetable condiment kimchee, and prefer it with dishes where the spicy pickle is paired with something smoky and sweet. It's a great complement to barbecued pork ribs and black-eyed peas, pulled pork on a soft bun with a sweet sauce, or even with hot dogs or pork chops (page 139). This way, the kimchee really sings and showcases the spicy and briny flavor in its full glory. My sous chef, Jung Song (aka Esther) Paek, taught me and my cooks at Orson about how much passion Koreans have for food, their pride in kimchee, and how to make many different versions. Surprisingly, I like it spicier than Esther does. If you leave the seeds of the chiles out, the kimchee will be much less hot. This recipe has a little heat, but it won't make you cry. An extremely helpful hint is to wear latex gloves while cutting up hot chiles and not to touch anywhere on your body, especially your eyes. If you don't have any gloves on hand, you can rub olive oil on your hands to create a temporary barrier against the heat from the chiles. Make sure you wash your hands thoroughly after and refrain from touching your face at all for a few hours.

Try kimchee tossed with stone fruit such as peaches or plums in the summer or persimmon in the fall as a bright accompaniment to any roasted or grilled meat or fish.

MARINADE

1 pound baby bok choy or cabbage, coarsely chopped

3 tablespoons salt

2 teaspoons sugar

1 teaspoon Asian fish sauce

KIMCHEE

One 4-inch piece daikon radish, halved lengthwise and cut into very thin half-moon slices

1 medium carrot, cut into 1-inch matchsticks

1 medium jalapeño chile, stemmed and thinly sliced (you can leave the seeds in for extra heat or remove the seeds for milder kimchee)

1 or 2 small Thai chiles, stemmed and seeded, if desired (depending on how hot you like it), thinly sliced

$1/4$ cup minced onion

4 cloves garlic, minced

4 teaspoons peeled and grated fresh ginger

4 teaspoons sugar

4 teaspoons Asian fish sauce

$1/2$ to 1 teaspoon cayenne pepper (optional)

○ For the marinade, in a large bowl, combine the bok choy, salt, sugar, and fish sauce. Cover and set aside at room temperature in a cool area for 8 to 10 hours.

○ For the kimchee, rinse the bok choy under cold running water and drain. In a separate large bowl, combine the rest of the ingredients and then toss with the drained bok choy. Cover again and set aside at room temperature in a cool area for 3 to 4 days. It will stink because of the fermented radish and fish sauce, but it is supposed to. Kimchee keeps indefinitely, covered in an airtight container in the refrigerator, or until you eat it all.

MAYONNAISE

Whether you whisk by hand or make it in a food processor, it is important to add the canola oil in a slow and steady stream so the mayonnaise fully emulsifies. You can use all canola oil, but I like the taste of a few spoonfuls of olive oil added at the end for a clean flavor.

MAKES ABOUT ³/₄ CUP

1 large egg, coddled (page 12)

¹/₄ teaspoon sugar

1 teaspoon salt

1 teaspoon Dijon mustard

1¹/₂ teaspoons freshly squeezed lemon juice or white wine vinegar

¹/₂ cup canola oil

2 tablespoons olive oil

○ Crack the egg into a small bowl and whisk in the sugar, salt, mustard, and lemon juice. Slowly whisk in the canola oil until the mixture emulsifies. Whisk in the olive oil. Adjust the seasoning if necessary. The mayonnaise will keep in an airtight container in the refrigerator for up to 1 month.

Note: If your mayonnaise breaks, add a drop or two of water and whisk to emulsify.

Roasted TOMATO–CHIPOTLE SALSA

Think of this as a pumped-up tomato sauce. It's great for dipping or as a zippy alternative to all the ways you would use a traditional tomato sauce. I prefer using dry-farmed tomatoes if you can find them, because they have a more concentrated flavor. They have been grown without being watered, usually in volcanic mineral-rich soil, where they get moisture from the earth.

MAKES ABOUT 4 CUPS

1 chipotle chile, or 2 teaspoons pure chipotle chile powder, or 1 teaspoon pimentón (Spanish smoked paprika) plus 1 teaspoon pure ancho chile powder

1/2 cup water

6 to 8 dry-farmed tomatoes

2 cloves garlic, chopped

1/2 jalapeño chile, seeded and chopped

1/2 red onion, chopped

1 tablespoon freshly squeezed lime juice

1/4 cup minced fresh cilantro

Dash of hot sauce (such as Cholula or Tapatio)

1 tablespoon salt

Freshly ground black pepper

○ If using a whole chipotle chile, bring the 1/2 cup water to a boil, add the dried chile, cover, and remove from the heat. Set aside for 15 minutes to rehydrate. Remove and discard the stem and seeds.

○ On a grill or over a direct flame, char the tomatoes for about 2 minutes on each side. Or, preheat the broiler to the highest setting, put the tomatoes on a baking sheet, and broil, turning once, until the skin is blackened, 4 to 5 minutes per side. Set the tomatoes aside to cool. Add the chipotle chile, tomatoes, garlic, jalapeño, onion, lime juice, cilantro, and hot sauce to the bowl of a food processor and pulse for about 30 seconds until a coarse puree is formed. Season with salt and pepper.

○ Keep in an airtight container in the refrigerator for up to a week.

STEAK Sauce

I came up with this steak sauce to serve with a burger. It's really like a spicy substitute for ketchup. A few spoonfuls, some Cobb Relish (page 18), and a little Mayonnaise (page 22) elevates a good burger into something truly great.

MAKES ABOUT 1¹/₂ CUPS

2 teaspoons red pepper flakes

1 tablespoon warm water

¹/₄ cup molasses

¹/₄ cup honey

1 tablespoon garlic powder

3 tablespoons soy sauce

1 tablespoon Worcestershire sauce

2 tablespoons ketchup

1 tablespoon mustard powder

2 tablespoons grated fresh horseradish

3 tablespoons bourbon

○ In a small bowl, rehydrate the red pepper flakes in the 1 tablespoon warm water and set aside for 5 minutes.

○ Combine the molasses, honey, garlic, soy sauce, Worcestershire, ketchup, mustard, horseradish, and bourbon in a blender and puree for 1 minute. Add the rehydrated red pepper flakes and water, transfer to a saucepan with the molasses mixture, and bring to a boil over medium heat. Remove from the heat and set aside to cool completely. Store in an airtight container in the refrigerator for up to 3 months.

TAHINI Sauce

I have learned so much over many years from my relationships with other chefs and food experts. Joyce Goldstein, a San Francisco Bay Area restaurateur and culinary leader, is one of these people. She is a consultant to so many food and restaurant-related projects and an expert in Mediterranean cooking and beyond, which she showcased in her acclaimed San Francisco restaurant, Square One, and in her many cookbooks. My tahini sauce is adapted from hers. I love it because the tahini acts as the fat and you don't need any other oil. Also, it is so pungent with garlic and spice that no vinegar is needed either. A splash of lemon juice and water are the liquid. You can find tahini at Middle Eastern markets and at most markets. This sauce is a must for Falafel (page 156).

MAKES 1/2 CUP

1/4 cup tahini (sesame seed puree)

1 clove garlic

1/2 teaspoon cumin seed, toasted and ground

1/4 teaspoon fennel seed, toasted and ground

3/4 teaspoon salt

1 tablespoon freshly squeezed lemon juice

1/4 teaspoon cayenne pepper or a pure chile powder such as Urfa or ancho

2 to 3 tablespoons water

○ In a food processor, combine the tahini, garlic, ground cumin and fennel seed, salt, lemon juice, and cayenne. Pulse until smooth. With the motor running, add the water slowly until a creamy dressing comes together.

TOMATO Sauce

I make tomato sauce often. I make a batch to use that same night, and freeze what is left over to pull out and cook with when I want to throw something together quickly, like a grilled pizza or a pasta. A ricer or food mill is an inexpensive piece of kitchen equipment and there are many sizes. This is the best way to puree this sauce.

MAKES ABOUT 3¹/₂ CUPS

2 tablespoons olive oil

1 medium onion, chopped

4 cloves garlic, minced

1 teaspoon dried oregano

1 Fresno chile, minced, or ¹/₂ teaspoon red pepper flakes

1 (28-ounce) can whole tomatoes, such as San Marzano, with half of the juice strained out, and crushed with your fingers

2 tablespoons tomato paste

Salt and freshly ground black pepper

○ Add the olive oil to a large saucepan over high heat; decrease the heat to medium. Add the onion and cook for 1 minute, stirring often, until the onion begins to soften. Add the garlic, oregano, and chile, and stir to mix. Add the crushed tomatoes, tomato paste, a large pinch of salt, and a few cranks of pepper. Decrease the heat to medium-low and cook for about 8 to 10 minutes. Run the tomato sauce through a ricer, otherwise known as a food mill, break up the tomatoes with a few pulses of an immersion blender, or use as is. Taste and season with more salt and pepper, if needed.

Walnut-Basil PESTO

Pesto was so trendy in the 1980s and, like much that is in fashion, it went out of style. But it's back! And when made fresh, it is divine on pastas and pizza as well as with fish or chicken. I add Parmesan or pecorino cheese only at the end of preparing pasta dishes or pizza, meaning, I don't add cheese to the pesto but rather after I have tossed the pasta with the pesto or spread it on a pizza. Walnuts are one of the healthiest nuts and the flavor is great with basil. Blanching the garlic takes out some of the bite and makes the pesto more rounded in flavor.

MAKES ABOUT 1 CUP

$1/2$ cup water

4 cloves garlic, coarsely chopped

2 cups loosely packed fresh basil leaves

Heaping $1/2$ cup walnut halves

1 teaspoon salt

Freshly ground black pepper

$1/2$ teaspoon grated lemon zest

$1/2$ to $3/4$ cup olive oil

○ In a small saucepan, bring the $1/2$ cup water to a boil and drop in the garlic for 30 seconds. Drain and rinse the garlic under cold water.

○ Have an ice bath (a bowl of ice water) ready. Bring a large pot of water to a boil over high heat, blanch the basil leaves for 30 to 45 seconds, and then immediately transfer the basil to the ice bath. Drain. Squeeze out any excess water and coarsely chop the basil.

○ In a blender, combine the blanched garlic, walnuts, basil, salt, pepper, lemon zest, and half of the olive oil. Puree until smooth and slowly add the rest of the olive oil. Stored in an airtight container, the pesto will keep for 1 week in the refrigerator and up to 3 months in the freezer.

Condiments and Basics

CROSTINI, Two Ways

Italian for "little toasts," crostini are slices of toasted rustic bread that are delicious simply brushed with olive oil, slathered with a spread (I love it with Harissa, page 19), or finished any number of ways. I enjoy them topped with scrambled eggs all year, or layered with summer's best tomatoes, sliced garlic, and fragrant fresh basil. Cut into cubes, they become croutons, bite-size morsels that add a crunchy dimension to salads. These are best used the day they are made but can be kept in an airtight container for a few days.

MAKES ABOUT 60 CROSTINI, OR 8 CUPS $1/2$-INCH-SQUARE CROUTONS

1 baguette or other hearth bread, preferably day old

$1/4$ cup olive oil

1 to 2 teaspoons salt

○ Preheat the oven to 375°F.

○ **For crostini:** Cut the bread into $1/4$-inch-thick slices, trimming off the ends. Spread the slices on a baking sheet. Drizzle or brush the slices with olive oil. Sprinkle with salt. Toast in the oven until browned and crunchy, 15 to 20 minutes. Cool completely.

○ **For croutons:** Cut the bread into $1/2$-inch cubes. Toss in a bowl with the olive oil and salt and spread out on a baking sheet. Toast in the oven until browned and crunchy, 20 to 25 minutes. Cool completely.

Crunchy BREAD CRUMBS

Bread crumbs are a quick way to add a little crunch to a dish. Panko are Japanese bread crumbs made from dried white bread. Panko bread crumbs are larger than other bread crumbs and have enough surface area that when cooked in a little oil, lend an extra fantastic crunchiness to top everything from pastas to eggs (and just about anything else).

MAKES ABOUT $1/2$ CUP

2 tablespoons olive oil

$1/2$ cup panko (Japanese dried bread crumbs) or other dried bread crumbs

$1/2$ teaspoon salt

$1/4$ teaspoon minced fresh thyme or rosemary

○ Add the olive oil to a sauté pan and heat over high heat. Add the bread crumbs, salt, and thyme and sauté, stirring constantly, until the crumbs get nice and toasty-crunchy golden brown. Immediately remove from the pan and let cool.

Condiments and Basics

STOCKS

There are two basic ways to make stocks: One is that you bring all the raw ingredients to a boil and then simmer for an hour or more, skimming off the impurities that rise to the top of the pot. The other is to brown the bones and vegetables, bring all to a boil with water, and simmer for an hour or so, skimming off the impurities that rise to the top of the pot. I have a method that is a little of both. I usually make stock at home after I roast a chicken, so I use the roasted chicken carcass and then I add raw vegetables, spices, and herbs to the pot (the aromatics), and water to cover. You can also decide whether you want to use other aromatics such as ginger and star anise in your chicken stock or cloves or allspice in your beef stock. It depends on what you like. If I think I am going on a ramen kick, I will want my chicken stock to have more Asian flavors, so I might add ginger and star anise and Szechuan peppercorns. Also, in place of the chicken bones, you can use duck bones for duck stock or pork bones for pork stock, or lamb bones in place of the beef bones for lamb stock.

CHICKEN Stock

MAKES 4 TO 6 CUPS

2 pounds chicken bones (necks, backs, and feet are great) or 1 roasted chicken carcass, meat picked off

1 white or yellow onion

3 ribs celery, coarsely chopped

2 carrots, cut into chunks

1 leek, coarsely chopped and rinsed

1 teaspoon peppercorns

1 bay leaf

3 sprigs thyme

4 sprigs Italian parsley

○ To roast fresh chicken bones, preheat the oven to 400°F. Put the bones on a baking sheet and roast for about 45 minutes. Drain off the excess grease and discard or store it in the refrigerator to cook with another time.

○ Combine all the ingredients in a large stockpot and cover with water (about 12 cups). Bring to a boil over high heat, skim off any foam that rises to the surface, and decrease the heat to a simmer. Cook, uncovered, for 1½ hours.

○ Strain and chill. Remove any solidified fat from the surface before using. I keep stock covered in the refrigerator for up to 1 week and in the freezer for up to 3 months.

BEEF Stock

MAKES 4 TO 6 CUPS

2 pounds beef bones (preferably marrow
    bones)

2 yellow onions, with skin, coarsely chopped

2 carrots, cut into chunks

3 ribs celery, coarsely chopped

5 cloves garlic

3 sprigs thyme

4 sprigs Italian parsley

1 tablespoon tomato paste

1 tablespoon whole black peppercorns

1 tablespoon salt

1 cup white or red wine

○ To roast fresh beef bones, preheat the oven to 400°F. Put the bones on a baking sheet and roast for about 45 minutes. Drain off the excess grease and discard.

○ Combine all the ingredients in a large stockpot and cover with water (about 12 cups). Bring to a boil over high heat, skim off any foam that rises to the surface, and decrease the heat to a simmer. Cook, uncovered, for $1^{1}/_{2}$ hours.

○ Strain and chill. Remove any solidified fat from the surface before using. I keep stock covered in the refrigerator for up to 1 week and in the freezer for up to 3 months.

SALADS IN 3-D

WHAT I WANT is a salad that delivers a lot of satisfaction. It doesn't need many ingredients, sometimes all I need is just a few handfuls of arugula gently tossed with a simple squeeze of lemon juice, a pinch of salt, and a drizzle of olive oil. In this case it's about letting just those ingredients sing together. Sometimes I want to make salads based on seasonal ingredients and, as with any recipe, travel somewhere fun with those ingredients. The salads in this chapter have more than a few ingredients and are oftentimes about balancing extreme flavors and textures.

Ultimately, a salad is about a balance of acidity (such as lemon juice or vinegar or fruit), fat (such as olive or nut oils), salt (which is, of course, salt, but could also come from the saltiness of cheese or olives), and sugar (from fruit and sometimes a touch of honey or syrup in a vinaigrette). I refer to this as something similar to sound mixing, where I want to turn up or turn down the volume of a flavor with other accents. I end up composing a few more accents or flavors and textures in my salads. More often, I want a lot of color in a salad as well as dramatic flavor and texture. The most important

34

thing is to taste what you are working with first. If the apples have a lot of sourness, you might add a little more sweetness. Also, if a cheese is really salty, start with less salt in the vinaigrette. **Using seasonal ingredients wherever you live is the best advice I can give you**, and if you live in a place where other greens, fruits, and vegetables grow, try substituting ones that seem like they might work in one of these recipes. This is how I have adapted to the randomness of cooking in competition, where a different ingredient is presented and I think, well that is similar to . . . so I will taste as I go.

All of these salads are great as starters but can easily be a **meal on their own.** And all of them are total crowd-pleasers. They're personal favorites, including some twists and turns on classic and iconic salads. The original cobb salad is great, but better when it is tomato focused. I love a classic poached egg lardon salad but have changed it up with spinach and potatoes. Niçoise salad is a classic, and I have given it a little more punch with saffron and a tomato broth that complements the textural contrast of almonds and olives.

Tomato-Centric COBB SALAD

There's nothing *wrong* with the classic cobb salad, but a few tweaks on the ingredients and using more tomatoes in season makes this unforgettable.

An inventive California restaurateur with too many leftovers is credited with creating this iconic salad in the 1920s. My version gives a nod to the original, with many of the same ingredients, but gets updated with modern flavors like crème fraîche and peppery greens. There's a sense of discovery in each bite: tomato with blue cheese or bacon with avocado and egg. Chicken is traditional in a cobb salad, but I don't think it's necessary (you can add some if you like). Here, protein is represented by the egg. I prefer lots of tomatoes in season for my version—more than usual—and instead of a vinaigrette, there's a creamy blue cheese dressing that recalls the crumbled blue cheese of the original recipe. The tarragon provides a high, licorice-y fennel note that helps the salad sing.

SERVES 4

2 slices bacon, cut into $1/2$-inch pieces

4 Croutons (page 28), crumbled, or Crunchy Bread Crumbs (page 29)

Squeeze of lemon juice

$1/4$ cup crème fraîche or sour cream

1 tablespoon finely chopped fresh tarragon

2 tablespoons crumbled blue cheese (such as Maytag or Point Reyes Blue)

Salt and freshly ground black pepper

2 large heirloom tomatoes, cut into slices, or 1 cup cherry tomatoes, halved

1 cup arugula or mâche greens, or 8 leaves romaine lettuce, chopped into $3/4$-inch-wide ribbons (chiffonade)

1 ripe avocado, peeled, pitted, and sliced

2 large Medium-Boiled Eggs (page 12), peeled and halved

○ Heat a small sauté pan over high heat. Add the bacon pieces to the hot pan and decrease the heat to low. Cook the bacon until crispy, then toss the croutons with the bacon and its rendered bacon fat; add a squeeze of lemon juice. Remove from the heat and set aside.

○ For the blue cheese dressing, combine the crème fraîche with the tarragon and blue cheese in a bowl and whisk until smooth; season with salt and pepper.

○ To assemble the salad, season the tomatoes with salt. Smear a large spoonful of the dressing onto each plate. Toss the greens in the remaining dressing and divide among the plates. Add the tomatoes, avocado slices, and 1 egg half to each plate. Top with the croutons and bacon and finish with some pepper. Serve immediately.

Roasted and Raw CARROT SALAD with AVOCADO and Toasted CUMIN VINAIGRETTE

I love using baby carrots in assorted colors. Thumbelina carrots, which are little and stubby, are great for roasting. I use red, orange, yellow, and white carrots for the ribbons, which make this salad so vibrant. Even just the orange variety next to the green of the avocado and mizuna makes a beautiful and colorful salad. Toasting whole cumin seeds and then grinding them in a mortar and pestle or an electric spice grinder is essential for the great taste of this vinaigrette. If you don't have either way of grinding spices, you can substitute cumin powder. This salad rocks from the contrast between the soft texture and caramelized sweetness of the roasted carrots and their raw and crunchy counterparts.

SERVES 4

2 bunches (about 10 ounces total) baby carrots in assorted colors, tops trimmed

1/4 cup olive oil, plus more as needed

Salt and freshly ground black pepper

1/4 cup pine nuts

1 teaspoon cumin seeds

2 tablespoons freshly squeezed lemon juice

1 teaspoon freshly squeezed lime juice

1 ripe avocado

2 cups mizuna, watercress, ancho cress, or arugula greens

○ Preheat the oven to 375°F.

○ Have an ice bath (a bowl of ice water) ready. Using a vegetable peeler, peel ribbons of carrots from half of the carrots. Place in the ice water to chill (the ribbons will curl after a while in the water).

○ Place the remaining whole carrots on a baking sheet; drizzle with some olive oil and season with salt and pepper. Roast until the edges start to caramelize, 15 to 20 minutes. Remove from the oven and set aside at room temperature. Lower the oven temperature to 350°F.

○ Toast the pine nuts in the oven for about 10 minutes or in a small pan on the stove top over medium-low heat, shaking constantly, until brown and fragrant; pour into a bowl to cool and set aside. Toast the cumin seeds in a small sauté pan over medium heat, tossing or stirring constantly until fragrant, and then pour quickly into a mortar and pestle or spice grinder and grind into a powder. Alternatively, use ground cumin.

○ For the dressing, in a medium bowl, whisk the cumin with the lemon and lime juices, salt, and pepper; slowly whisk in the 1/4 cup olive oil.

(continued)

○ Remove the carrot ribbons from the ice water and pat dry with paper towels. Peel, pit, and slice the avocado.

○ Divide the avocado slices and roasted carrots among 4 salad plates. In a bowl, toss the carrot ribbons and greens in the dressing, and divide among the plates.

○ Sprinkle a few pine nuts on each salad and serve.

Shaved SUMMER SQUASH with EGG, Toasted PINE NUTS, and PROSCIUTTO

We are spoiled in California for many reasons, but especially in the bounty of fresh produce available to us, including the many kinds of squash. Varietals of summer squash grow all over the United States. Summer squash is the term we use for all squashes including zucchini. There are yellow crookneck, Rond de Nice, Black Beauties, golden zucchini, Peter Pan, pattypan, and lots more. Use whatever you can find! Everyone thinks of zucchini as a common roasted or grilled vegetable, but I think it is best served raw, cooked only by salt and acid, and dressed in a little olive oil. The addition of the crunchy bread crumbs, egg, and prosciutto make this a substantial salad.

SERVES 2

2 yellow summer squash or zucchini (or 1 of each), or 4 small pattypan, crookneck, or Ronde de Nice squash

Salt and freshly ground black pepper

2 tablespoons freshly squeezed lemon juice

3 tablespoons olive oil

8 leaves fresh basil or mint (or 4 of each)

2 tablespoons Crunchy Bread Crumbs (page 29)

2 large Medium-Boiled Eggs (page 12), peeled and halved

6 slices prosciutto

4 tablespoons toasted pine nuts

Cracked black pepper, for finishing

○ With a vegetable peeler, shave ribbons of whatever summer squash you have. Season with salt. Add the lemon juice, olive oil, and basil. Toss gently and divide between 2 plates. Sprinkle the squash with the bread crumbs. Arrange 2 egg halves on top of the bread crumbs, and place 3 slices of prosciutto on each plate. Finish with the pine nuts and some cracked pepper. Serve immediately.

Warm SPINACH SALAD LARDON with Roasted YUKON GOLD POTATOES and MUSTARD VINAIGRETTE

The traditional poached egg–lardon salad uses frisée—a feathery green in the chicory family with a slightly bitter flavor. Lardon refers to the fat-cut pieces of cured pork belly, not usually smoked like bacon is, but I like bacon with this. The spinach is tossed quickly in the vinaigrette with the bacon, and roasted Yukon gold potatoes to soak up more of the mustard vinaigrette. This is a meal of a salad and great for serving day or night.

SERVES 2

1 large Yukon gold potato (about 8 ounces), peeled and cut into medium dice

3 tablespoons olive oil

Salt and freshly ground black pepper

4 slices bacon or salt pork, cut into $^1/_2$-inch pieces

2 tablespoons whole-grain mustard

1 tablespoon Dijon mustard

2 tablespoons sherry vinegar

Squeeze of lemon juice

6 loosely packed cups baby spinach leaves

2 large Poached Eggs (page 13)

Fleur de sel (French sea salt), for finishing

○ Preheat the oven to 350°F.

○ Toss the potato with 1 tablespoon of the olive oil and some salt, and spread on a baking sheet. Roast until cooked through, tossing halfway through, 25 to 30 minutes. Set aside.

○ Meanwhile, heat a large sauté pan over high heat. Decrease the heat to medium-low and cook the bacon for about 5 minutes, stirring a few times. You want the bacon to still be soft and not crisp. Remove the bacon to drain on paper towels, but save the rendered fat in the pan.

○ In a bowl, whisk the mustards, vinegar, squeeze of lemon, and salt and pepper to taste with the remaining 2 tablespoons olive oil. Increase the heat to high under the sauté pan with the bacon fat; when very hot, add the roasted potatoes, the vinaigrette, and the spinach and toss quickly for 10 to 15 seconds. Remove and divide between 2 serving bowls or plates.

○ Top each serving with the reserved bacon and a poached egg. Finish with a pinch of *fleur de sel* and pepper on each poached egg. Serve immediately.

Salads in 3-D

Baby GREENS, Shaved MUSHROOMS, and WALNUT SALAD with PARMESAN and BLACK TRUFFLE–RED WINE VINAIGRETTE

I am not the kind of chef who works very much with truffles. My restaurants are more casual than fine dining. However I went to Parma, Italy, several times years ago when I was working with Barilla, the pasta company. Truffles were in season on a few of those trips and they seemed to be shaved on just about everything. Those trips spoiled me for truffles, but importing truffles to the United States is a big expense for chefs to pass along to our guests. However, farmers and entrepreneurs in this country are attempting to cultivate truffles and there is hope for a more affordable truffle some day, even from California. I do use truffle oil in mayonnaise for a burger sometimes, and I prefer black truffle paste for this salad, for the unequivocal taste of the earthy and luxurious truffle. With truffle paste, a little goes a long way. It is available in Italian delis and specialty markets as well as Whole Foods Market.

SERVES 4

1 small shallot, minced

2 tablespoons black truffle paste

1/2 tablespoon honey

3 tablespoons red wine vinegar

1 teaspoon salt

Freshly ground black pepper

1/4 cup olive oil

2 tablespoons walnut oil

About 8 cups torn mixed baby lettuces (such as Lola Rosa, red oak leaf, Little Gem, or baby romaine)

1 cup cremini mushrooms, cleaned and thinly shaved on a mandoline

1/2 cup walnut halves, toasted

1/4 cup shaved Parmegiano-Reggiano cheese

○ For the dressing, in a bowl combine the shallot, truffle paste, honey, and vinegar. Add the salt and pepper. Whisk in the olive oil and the walnut oil.

○ Toss the lettuce in half of the dressing and divide among 4 plates. Cover the greens with the mushrooms and walnuts, and drizzle with the remaining vinaigrette. Top with the shaved cheese and serve immediately.

ARUGULA SALAD with APPLES, Toasted PECANS, and BLUE CHEESE

I have an obsession with the combination of apples, blue cheese, and pecans. This trinity shows up often in my desserts and salads. I discovered Steen's cane syrup, made from sugar cane, when I was in New Orleans a few years ago, and use it in the dressing. It tastes like caramelized sugar with a little bitterness to cut the sweetness. You can get Steen's cane syrup online. You can also substitute maple syrup for the cane syrup or half the amount in molasses, as it is much stronger in flavor. This is a great fall salad. Jewel-like pomegranate seeds make it even more beautiful, so add them when they show up in produce markets.

SERVES 2

1 tablespoon cane syrup

2 tablespoons freshly squeezed lemon juice

1 teaspoon salt

Freshly ground black pepper

3 tablespoons olive oil

1 crisp apple (such as Mutsu, Jonagold, or Gravenstein), halved, cored, and sliced (skin left on)

4 cups arugula

$^1/_2$ cup toasted pecans

$^1/_4$ cup (about 2 ounces) crumbled blue cheese (such as Point Reyes Blue, Gorgonzola, or Stilton)

$^1/_4$ cup pomegranate seeds (optional)

○ In a bowl, combine the cane syrup, lemon juice, salt, and a few cranks of black pepper. Whisk in the olive oil. Add the apples to the bowl along with the arugula and pecans and toss together gently. Divide between 2 salad plates. Sprinkle with the blue cheese and pomegranate seeds. Add more pepper if desired.

○ Serve immediately.

Note: To get pomegranate seeds free from the skin and membranes, cut the pomegranate in half and, with a wooden spoon, smack the back side of the skin to release the seeds. You will still have to pull apart some of the membrane walls to get all the seeds out. Keep unused pomegranate seeds in a covered container in the refrigerator for up to 4 days.

BLOOD ORANGE SALAD with FENNEL, OLIVES, ALMONDS, and RICOTTA SALATA

This is a gorgeous salad with a variety of textures. The dry-cured olives are both salty and fruity and a great contrast to the crunch of almonds and licorice flavor of fennel. Then you get the gush of the fruity, citrusy, blood oranges, balanced with a touch of honey and the gorgeous orange blossom water. The whole thing is finished with a snowfall of grated ricotta salata. Orange blossom water is found at Middle Eastern markets and also at specialty and Whole Foods Markets.

SERVES 2 TO 4

1 small bulb fennel

3 blood oranges

2 teaspoons sherry vinegar

$^1/_4$ teaspoon orange blossom water

$^1/_2$ teaspoon honey

Pinch of salt

2 tablespoons olive oil

2 cups arugula or watercress

$^1/_4$ cup whole roasted almonds

8 dry-cured black olives, pitted and torn in half

1 ounce ricotta salata cheese, shaved or crumbled

○ Have an ice bath (a bowl of ice water) ready. With a mandoline, shave the fennel thinly, or slice very thinly with a sharp knife, and drop the pieces into the ice bath. Cut the rind off of each orange by cutting off the ends first and then tracing the round shape of the orange to cut off the rind and the pith and remove all of the skin around the oranges. Cut the peeled oranges into 1/4-inch-thick slices or carefully cut out the peeled segments from between the membranes with a sharp knife. Arrange the orange slices on plates. Drain the shaved fennel and pat dry with paper towels.

○ For the dressing, in a bowl, whisk the vinegar, orange blossom water, honey, and salt together. Whisk in the olive oil.

○ Toss the arugula, shaved fennel, and almonds with 2 spoonfuls of the vinaigrette and arrange on top of the orange slices. Divide the olives among each salad and finish with shavings or crumbles of the ricotta salata cheese. Serve immediately.

Roasted BABY BEETS, Seared STEAK CARPACCIO, and HORSERADISH CREAM SALAD

Sometimes I want the taste of beef, but I don't want a large portion, which is why I love beef carpaccio. A little marinade and a sear on the beef rounds out the lightness and clean taste of raw beef and gives off a bit of umami, or savory. Along with roasted beets, tangy horseradish cream, crispy fried shallots, and some mâche greens make this is a great starter and a great anytime salad. It's a gorgeous dish and is bright and refreshing. The longest wait is for roasting the beets; otherwise, everything is easy to prepare.

SERVES 2

4 ounces fillet of beef or strip loin of beef

1 tablespoon Worcestershire sauce

1 teaspoon salt, plus more for seasoning

Freshly ground black pepper

6 baby beets, tops removed

1 tablespoon olive oil

1 tablespoon balsamic vinegar

1/4 teaspoon finely grated lemon zest

2 cups canola or peanut oil

1/4 cup cornstarch

1/4 cup rice flour

1/4 teaspoon cayenne pepper

1/4 cup buttermilk

1 shallot, thinly sliced, separated into rings

3 tablespoons crème fraîche

2 teaspoons grated fresh horseradish

1 cup mâche or arugula (preferably wild arugula)

Squeeze of lemon juice

Extra-virgin olive oil, for drizzling

○ Preheat the oven to 400°F.

○ In a small bowl, season the beef with the Worcestershire sauce, salt, and pepper and set aside for 15 to 20 minutes.

○ Place the baby beets in a roasting pan and toss with the 1 tablespoon olive oil and some salt and pepper. Cover with a tight-fitting lid or place everything in aluminum foil and wrap tightly. Roast until the beets can be pierced with a knife but are not super soft, 45 minutes to 1 hour. Remove from the oven and let cool slightly. The skins should slip off fairly easily, or use a paring knife to remove the skins. Cut each beet in half and toss in a bowl with the balsamic vinegar and lemon zest; season with salt and pepper. Set aside at room temperature.

(continued)

○ Meanwhile, pat the beef dry with a paper towel. Heat a cast-iron or other heavy skillet over high heat until smoking. Add the beef and cook for about 2 minutes on each side. Remove from the heat and let the beef rest for about 10 minutes (or you can do this earlier, wrap the seared beef, and chill until ready to eat). Cut the seared beef into $1/2$-inch slices. Put the slices between 2 pieces of plastic wrap or parchment paper. With a meat mallet or smooth pounder, or a rolling pin, pound out the beef slices until uniformly very thin. Keep chilled until ready to serve.

○ For the shallots, heat the canola oil in a deep-sided pot to 375°F on a deep-fat thermometer. Combine the cornstarch, rice flour, the 1 teaspoon salt, and the cayenne in a shallow bowl. Pour the buttermilk into another shallow bowl. Dredge the sliced shallots in the cornstarch mixture and transfer them to a fine-mesh strainer, shaking off the excess cornstarch. Drop the coated shallots into the buttermilk and dredge again in the cornstarch mixture. Shake again to remove excess cornstarch. Drop the shallots into the hot oil, in batches if necessary, and fry until golden and crispy, 2 to 3 minutes. Drain on a clean kitchen towel or paper towel.

○ Mix the crème fraîche with the horseradish.

○ Divide the chilled carpaccio slices between 2 plates. Scatter the beet halves on top. Drizzle the crème fraîche mixture over the carpaccio. Toss the mâche with the lemon juice and divide between the plates. Scatter some fried shallots on each plate, drizzle with the extra-virgin olive oil, and grind more black pepper over if desired. Serve immediately.

My CHINESE CHICKEN SALAD with CRISP WONTONS and PLUM-GINGER VINAIGRETTE

Growing up in the Los Angeles area, I was exposed to a lot of Chinese chicken salad. I believe Wolfgang Puck first made it a classic L.A. salad at Chinois on Main in Venice Beach. Usually made with lettuce and/or cabbage, ginger-soy vinaigrette, shredded or grilled chicken, almonds or peanuts, and crispy fried rice noodles or wontons, it is a salad that combines lots of bright Asian flavors and is fun to eat. A favorite version was on the menu at Chin Chin, a trendy Chinese restaurant. My friend Cherie and I would eat there at least every week. There are many recipes for this Cal-Asian salad and now you can get it all over the place, even at airports. I have endless interpretations of this salad. I like matching the vinaigrette to the season: citrus vinaigrette in winter, rhubarb-ginger in spring, peach or plum in the summer, and Concord grape in fall. This version features plums.

For the citrus version, simply replace the plums with 1 cup of grapefruit and orange segments, and puree half of the citrus with the sugar, rice wine vinegar, and ginger without cooking the mixture. Use the other half of the grapefruit and orange segments to arrange on the salads.

SERVES 2

2 cups Chicken Stock (page 30)

1 clove garlic, smashed

1 knob fresh ginger, sliced

1 teaspoon peeled and grated fresh ginger (grated with a Microplane)

4 green onions, chopped (save root ends and trimmed tops for the poaching liquid)

1/2 teaspoon Szechuan peppercorns

1 whole star anise

1 cinnamon stick

2 tablespoons soy sauce

2 boneless skinless chicken breast halves (6 ounces each)

1/4 cup Mayonnaise (page 22)

1 tablespoon peanut butter

2 drops toasted sesame oil

1 teaspoon Sriracha hot sauce

2 plums (preferably Santa Rosa or Satsuma), halved, pitted, and sliced

Pinch of sugar

2 teaspoons rice wine vinegar

2 tablespoons water

3 tablespoons canola oil

Pinch of salt

3 baby bok choy, root ends trimmed and heads halved lengthwise

1/4 cup mung bean sprouts

1/4 cup crispy fried wonton strips (see Note, following)

2 teaspoons roasted peanuts

1/2 teaspoon toasted sesame seed

10 fresh cilantro leaves

○ In a large saucepan, combine the stock, garlic, sliced ginger, green onion trimmings, peppercorns, anise, cinnamon stick, and soy sauce and bring to a boil over high heat. Turn off the heat and let the aromatics steep in the liquid for 30 minutes. Strain and set the liquid back on the heat. Bring to a simmer over mediou-low heat and add the chicken breasts. Decrease the heat to low, cover, and simmer for 3 minutes. Turn off the heat and the allow chicken to continue to slowly cook in the liquid for another 10 minutes. Remove the chicken from the liquid (leave the liquid in the pan) and chill. Increase the heat to medium-high and cook until the liquid is reduced by half; chill in an ice bath (bowl of ice water). Slice the chicken breasts into 1/2-inch slices and set in a container. Pour the cooled reduction over the chicken and keep refrigerated until ready to use.

○ For the peanut dressing, in a small bowl, combine the mayonnaise, peanut butter, sesame oil, and hot sauce until smooth. Set aside.

○ For the plum-ginger vinaigrette, in a small saucepan, combine half the plum slices, sugar, vinegar, and the 2 tablespoons water. Over medium-high heat bring just to a boil. Decrease the heat to a low and simmer, stirring occasionally, until the water has evaporated and the plums are softened, about 2 minutes. Remove from the heat and let cool. Add to a blender along with the grated ginger and 1 tablespoon of the canola oil and puree. Strain through a sieve and season to taste with salt.

○ In a large sauté pan over high heat, add the remaining 2 tablespoons canola oil; place the bok choy halves in the pan and sear on the cut side for about 1 minute. Season each piece with salt. Flip over, cover the pan, and cook for 30 seconds more. Remove the bok choy from the pan and set aside.

○ To serve, add a spoonful of the peanut sauce to each of 2 plates. Arrange 3 bok choy halves on each plate, and drizzle on a few drops of the plum-ginger vinaigrette. Toss the uncooked plum slices and mung bean sprouts with the remaining vinaigrette and arrange in the middle of each plate. Divide the poached chicken between each salad. Top with the crispy fried wonton strips, peanuts, chopped green onion, sesame seed, and cilantro.

○ Serve immediately.

Note: To make crispy fried wonton crisps, heat 2 cups canola oil in a small deep pan to 375°F on a deep-fat thermometer. Slice fresh wonton wrappers into thin strips and drop in small batches into the hot oil. Fry, stirring with a strainer, until light golden brown, 2 to 3 minutes. Transfer to a paper towel–lined plate to drain and immediately sprinkle with salt, if desired.

SERIOUS SOUPS

WHEN I MAKE SOUP at work, this is my mindset: I have got to make enough soup for a small army. I am not sure where that comes from, but most likely it was from my first cooking job at Café Claude, where I did actually have to make enough soup for 60 to 75 portions a day. At home, I don't make a big pot of soup. Instead, I prepare lots of stock and freeze it in smaller portions to use as a base anytime I want to make a quick soup.

These are some plays on classics. I prefer a clam chowder not thickened and without a roux. New England–style clam chowder is thick enough for me with the cream and potatoes, and I love the little clams to not get lost. On the other hand, there are many alternative ways to thicken a soup and two of my favorites are with cornmeal such as in the Corn Soup (page 67), where the soup is almost a hybrid of thick polenta and a corn soup, and with bread, particularly with grilled bread, which gives a little more flavor because of the char. Soup made with

seasonal ingredients is obviously the best idea, but I've included soups that are simply traditional crowd-pleasers that I have adapted with some **modern interpretations.** Here are some of my favorites—remodeled.

SPRING PEA SOUP with MINT and SHEEP'S MILK YOGURT

I grew up in Southern California but have lived in Northern California most of my adult life. I have driven Highway 101 ("the 101" to Angelenos) up and down the state many times. On those trips I always pass the Buellton exit for Solvang, just north of Santa Barbara, home since 1924 to the restaurant Pea Soup Andersen's. No, I never go there! I went when I was a kid and am shocked at how it is still there and can appreciate it on this deep American level, but I just look at the signs and have a nostalgia about the trips. I think, let's redo this soup completely! My pea soup is about that trip, that nostalgia, and the success of Andersen's soup, but expressed in a different way. Especially after the winter holidays, I love just the idea that fresh peas are coming, and I fantasize about the energy and newness of spring. This soup isn't a hearty, stick-to-your ribs version, but more of a tribute to the lightness and freshness of the spring season.

SERVES 2 TO 4

1/2 cup fresh mint leaves

1/4 cup plus 1 tablespoon olive oil

1 cup shelled fresh peas (reserve pods for the broth)

2 cups vegetable stock or Chicken Stock (page 30)

2 tablespoons unsalted butter

1/4 cup pearl onions, halved lengthwise

Salt and freshly ground black pepper

2 tablespoons sheep's milk yogurt, for garnish

Pea shoots or tendrils, for garnish (optional)

1 sprig tarragon, for garnish

○ For the mint oil, have an ice bath (a bowl of ice water) ready. Bring a saucepan of water to a boil over high heat. Blanch the mint leaves in the boiling water and transfer with a slotted spoon to the ice water for a few seconds. Squeeze out the water and puree the mint in a blender with 1/4 cup of the olive oil. Strain, cover, and set aside in the refrigerator. Mint oil will last in the refrigerator for a week.

○ For the pea pod broth, in a blender, puree the pea pods with the stock and strain.

○ In a medium saucepot over medium heat, add the remaining 1 tablespoons olive oil and the butter. Add the pearl onions and decrease the heat to low. Add the pea pod broth and a big pinch of salt, and simmer for 5 minutes. Add the peas and simmer another 3 minutes. Season with salt and pepper.

○ Ladle the soup into bowls. Set a spoonful of yogurt in the middle of each bowl, drizzle with the mint oil, top with the pea shoots and tarragon leaves, and serve immediately.

CLAM CHOWDER

I prefer the New England style of clam chowder (aka "white chowder") rather than the tomato-based Manhattan version (aka "red chowder"), though I am tempted to rethink that style also. This is the New England version with a detour through California because I add fennel to the soup and I don't thicken it. I believe a thicker soup makes sense in freezing cold weather but not in California, even in foggy San Francisco where it does get chilly, occasionally frosty, but for snowballs and sledding we must drive 190 miles northeast to the Sierra. Cream is an ingredient here because I love how it pairs with shellfish. And I think the fennel and the lightness of this broth are what make the clams stand out. Creamy, yet light, this is a very satisfying soup.

SERVES 2

1 tablespoon olive oil

2 slices bacon or salt pork, cut into $1/4$-inch pieces

1 onion, cut into small dice

1 rib celery, cut into small dice

1 bay leaf

1 clove garlic, minced

3 sprigs thyme

$1/2$ bulb fennel, halved lengthwise and thinly sliced (reserve fronds for garnish)

2 dozen clams

2 cups dry white wine

$1/2$ cup bottled clam juice

1 cup cream

1 cup whole milk

2 Yukon gold or russet potatoes, peeled and cut into large chunks, steamed or boiled until just tender

$1/2$ teaspoon Tabasco sauce

Chopped fresh Italian parsley, for garnish

Chopped fresh tarragon, leaves for garnish

○ Set a medium stockpot over high heat and add the olive oil. Add the bacon and cook for 1 minute. Add the chopped onion, celery, bay leaf, garlic, thyme, and fennel and cook for 2 minutes. Add the clams, white wine, and clam juice.

○ Heat the cream and milk in a separate saucepan just until warm and then add to the clam pot. Then, add the potatoes and Tabasco. When the clams open, in about 4 to 5 minutes, the soup is ready to serve. If some clams just will not open after another 2 minutes, discard them.

○ Ladle immediately into bowls and garnish with the parsley, tarragon, and fennel fronds.

PHO

Pho, pronounced: "fah," is a staple soup from Vietnam made with rice noodles and often beef or fish broth. The aromatics in this soup are what distinguish it from other noodle soups. You need star anise, Asian fish sauce, ginger, and a few other somewhat exotic ingredients, but after tasting this, you are going to want it more often than any ordinary soup. I have given you a few options below. Traditionally, the pho is finished with thinly sliced raw beef that poaches in the broth as you eat it. This soup is great with sliced seared pork tenderloin or even creamy tofu. You can use whatever stock you like. You must also use mung bean sprouts, Thai basil, and cilantro leaves, as they are not just beautiful garnishes but also essential to the marriage of flavors in this soul-warming soup. I love going to Mei Wah, a bustling Asian supermarket on Clement Street in San Francisco, for all these ingredients. It is mayhem, packed with busy shoppers pushing everyone out of the way to get the first and the best of all the ingredients. It's fantastic and feels like a Chinese version of Wall Street, only with food rather than stocks to buy and sell.

SERVES 2 TO 4

4 green onions, roots trimmed off and tops trimmed off about 1 inch

4 cups Beef Stock (page 31), Chicken Stock (page 30), or vegetable stock

1 stick Saigon cinnamon or other cinnamon

3 star anise

2-inch piece fresh ginger, sliced

1/2 teaspoon whole Szechuan peppercorns

1/4 cup cilantro stems

2 kefir lime leaves

4 ounces dried rice noodles

1/2 cup fresh snow peas

2 tablespoons Asian fish sauce

1 tablespoon soy sauce

Salt and freshly ground black pepper

1 cup mung bean sprouts

1/4 cup fresh whole Thai basil leaves, for garnish

1/4 cup fresh cilantro leaves, for garnish

1 Fresno chile, sliced, for garnish

1 lime, quartered

○ On a hot grill or a very hot pan or wok, grill or char the green onions for about 2 to 3 minutes on both sides. Set aside to cool slightly. Chop into 1/2-inch pieces.

○ In a medium stockpot, combine the stock with the cinnamon stick, star anise, ginger, peppercorns, cilantro stems, and kefir lime leaves. Bring to a boil over high heat, decrease the heat to medium, and simmer for 15 minutes.

○ Meanwhile, put the rice noodles in a bowl, cover with hot water, and soak for 15 minutes to rehydrate; set aside.

○ Strain the soup and return the liquid to the pot. Add the green onions, snow peas, fish sauce, and soy sauce to the soup. Season with salt and pepper.

○ Divide the noodles between 2 bowls (or 4). Ladle soup into each bowl, then top with the mung bean sprouts, basil, cilantro leaves, and chile. Serve with the lime wedges on the side to squeeze into the soup.

Variation

Divide 8 ounces thinly sliced flank steak, sliced seared pork tenderloin, or fresh tofu between the bowls of soup and let the broth poach the meat.

Another option is to add half a Soft-Boiled Egg (page 12) to each bowl.

MATZO BALL SOUP

I crave matzo ball soup fairly often, despite the fact that I have no faily recipe to brag about. I just love dumplings, and from all cultures. There is much discussion as to how to make the matzo balls light and tender. My secret—club soda and a light touch. I've taken a few liberties with this recipe—adding pearl onions, baby carrots, beets, and Toyko turnips—a small white variety of turnip. Basically, it's a matzo ball soup pumped up with lots of flavorful vegetables that would make any grandmother proud.

SERVES 2 TO 4

1 cup matzo meal

4 large eggs, lightly beaten

2 tablespoons rendered duck or chicken fat

3 ounces club soda

2 teaspoons kosher salt, plus more for seasoning

A few cranks black pepper, plus more for seasoning

$1/8$ teaspoon caraway seeds, toasted and ground

2 tablespoons vegetable oil

6 pearl onions, halved lengthwise

1 rib celery, cut into $1/2$-inch pieces

3 baby or Thumbelina carrots, quartered lengthwise

2 Tokyo turnips, halved lengthwise (optional or other turnips, cut into $1/2$-inch pieces

3 cups Chicken Stock (page 30)

2 roasted baby beets, halved lengthwise (optional, see page 47)

1 tablespoon minced fresh Italian parsley

○ In a medium bowl, combine the eggs, fat, and soda water and then add the matzo meal. Add the 2 teaspoons salt, a few cranks of black pepper, and the ground caraway. Stir all the ingredients together lightly with a spatula or a wooden spoon. Set aside in the refrigerator for 30 minutes. Bring a large pot of salted water to a boil over high heat. Form 1- to 2-inch balls of the mixture with your hands or a scoop. Do not compress or overwork the mixture or they will be tough. Decrease the heat to medium-high and drop the balls into the simmering water and cook for 25 minutes. Remove with a slotted spoon, drain, and set aside on a plate.

○ For the soup, add the vegetable oil to a saucepot set over high heat. Decrease the heat to low and add the pearl onions, celery, carrots, and turnips, and cook for 2 to 3 minutes. Add the stock and season with salt and pepper. Bring to a boil and decrease the heat to a simmer. Add the matzo balls to the soup and simmer for 5 minutes, or until the vegetable are tender.

○ To serve, spoon a few matzo balls into soup bowls and divide the vegetables and soup between the bowls. Add a couple of the roasted beet halves to each bowl and sprinkle with the parsley. Serve immediately.

WINTER SQUASH SOUP with APPLE BUTTER TOAST

Cold nights need comfort food. While winter squash soup doesn't sound sexy, the sweetness of the squash and a little apple and spice on toast is just the bit of something we need once in a while. I swear you will come back for more.

SERVES 2 TO 4

2 tablespoons olive oil

2 tablespoons unsalted butter

1¹/₂ cups kabocha or butternut squash, peeled, seeded, and cut into ¹/₂-inch cubes

¹/₂ yellow onion, cut into small dice

¹/₂ teaspoon curry powder

¹/₂ teaspoon coriander seeds or ground coriander

¹/₂ cup freshly squeezed orange juice

2 cups Chicken Stock (page 30)

1 to 2 cups water

Salt and freshly ground black pepper

1 cup peeled, chopped apples

¹/₂ cup sugar

1 cup apple cider

¹/₂ teaspoon ground cinnamon

¹/₄ teaspoon ground nutmeg

4 tablespoons crème fraîche

8 slices baguette or other hearth bread, toasted and buttered

○ For the soup, in a medium stockpot over high heat, add the olive oil and butter. Decrease the heat to medium and add the squash and onion and sauté for 3 to 4 minutes. Add the curry powder, coriander, orange juice, stock, and water along with a couple of heavy pinches of salt and some pepper. Simmer until the squash is tender, 20 to 30 minutes.

○ While the soup is cooking, make the apple butter. Combine the apples with the sugar, cider, cinnamon, and nutmeg in a saucepan and simmer over medium heat for 30 minutes. Set aside to cool.

○ Puree and strain the soup.

○ To serve, ladle the soup into bowl and garnish with the crème fraîche. Serve with the buttered toast topped with some apple butter.

MINESTRONE

I adore a perfect tomato-based soup with seasonal and regional vegetables and spices. Okay, we don't all have the same vegetables available all the time, but this soup is about what you have access to. It is something I feel like I have seen a lot of on menus over the decades. But I like to take what I've got and run with it. Let's say there are fresh green beans in the vegetable crisper and canned tomatoes in the pantry (or vice versa). What are their textures and flavors? What else do I have to give it some flash? Start with a base and build from there. Please swap whatever vegetables *you* may have for any of these ingredients. And grilled Italian bread rubbed with olive oil and garlic is the perfect partner with any version of minestrone you (or I) could come up with.

SERVES 2 TO 4

4 ounces dried cannellini, kidney, or navy beans, or 1 cup canned, drained and rinsed

2 tablespoons olive oil

1 yellow onion, cut into medium dice

1 carrot, cut into medium dice

2 ribs celery, cut into medium dice

3 cloves garlic, thinly sliced

1 Fresno chile, halved, seeded, and finely chopped, or 1/4 teaspoon red pepper flakes

2 teaspoons dried oregano

1/4 teaspoon pimentón dulce (mild Spanish paprika)

8 ounces canned (I prefer San Marzano) tomatoes

3 cups vegetable broth or Chicken Stock (page 30)

2 teaspoons salt

Freshly ground black pepper

1 cup haricots verts, stemmed and cut into 1/4-inch pieces, or 1/2 cup canned green beans drained, and cut into 1/4-inch pieces

2 tablespoons chopped fresh Italian parsley

Pecorino romano or Parmigiano-Reggiano cheese, for grating

○ Soak the dried beans in cold water overnight. Rinse and cook in 2 cups fresh water and 1/2 teaspoon salt in a saucepan over medium heat for about 30 minutes or until tender. Drain.

○ In a medium stockpot, add the olive oil over high heat. Add the onion, carrot, and celery and sauté for 2 minutes. Decrease the heat to low.

○ Add the garlic, chile, and oregano to the vegetable mixture. Add the pimentón and then the tomatoes. Add the stock, 2 teaspoons salt, and a few cranks of pepper and bring to a simmer. Add the cannellini beans and simmer for 15 to 20 minutes. Add the haricots verts or green beans and season to taste. Simmer for another 5 minutes.

○ Serve immediately, garnished with the chopped Italian parsley and grated pecorino or Parmesan.

CORN SOUP

When I was growing up, my grandparents had a farm outside of Joplin, Missouri. In the summer, my brother Jason and I would ride the tractor with my grandpa when he would plow the fields and corn would be growing tall. We would all pick corn for dinner, and I just love that smell of the corn pulled off the stalks and the memory of the plowed earth all around it. Nothing compares. I like corn in many savory and sweet dishes. It is sweet and starchy and blends well with other ingredients, which likely explains its popularity. This soup is based on fresh corn, thickened with a little cornmeal. But try pureeing thinned-out cooked grits or polenta with chicken stock. This earthy topping is a recreation of the smell and feeling I had as a kid standing in that corn field. I like this soup with the addition of sautéed mushrooms of any kind, but particularly black trumpet mushrooms because of their mysterious earthy flavor.

SERVES 2 TO 4

SOUP

1 tablespoon olive oil

2 tablespoons unsalted butter

1 yellow onion

4 ears summer corn, kernels cut off and cobs reserved

1 sprig thyme

2 sprigs tarragon

4 cups water

2 tablespoons cornmeal

Salt and freshly ground black pepper

TOPPING

2 tablespoons cacao nibs

$1/2$ teaspoon porcini mushroom powder

1 teaspoon black sesame seed

1 teaspoon turbinado sugar

$1/4$ teaspoon salt

1 teaspoon olive oil

2 drops truffle oil (optional)

2 tablespoons crème fraîche, for garnish

○ For the soup, in a medium stockpot, add the olive oil and butter over high heat. Add the onion, decrease the heat to medium, and cook for 2 to 3 minutes. Add the corn kernels and sauté for another minute. Add the cobs, thyme, tarragon, water, and cornmeal. Add a large pinch of salt and a few cranks of pepper and simmer for 20 to 30 minutes. Remove and discard the cobs. Puree the soup in a blender or in the pot with an immersion blender and season to taste.

○ While the soup is cooking, make the topping. Combine the nibs, porcini mushroom powder, sesame seed, sugar, salt, olive oil, and truffle oil in a food processor.

○ To serve, ladle the soup into bowls and garnish with the crème fraîche and the earthy topping. Serve immediately.

Grilled BREAD SOUP with CAVALO NERO and POACHED EGG

This soup is perfect for icy-cold nights and a great soup for the holidays. Flavorful grilled bread is the subtle thickener here. It's the kind of culinary magic that inspires guests to ask you how you ever thought to do that! Which is ironic, considering that cooks have been thickening soup with cooked or stale bread for, well, almost forever.

SERVES 2 TO 4

2 slices sourdough bread

4 tablespoons olive oil

1 teaspoon white wine or apple cider vinegar

2 slices bacon, cut into small dice

1 white or yellow onion, cut into small dice

1 carrot, cut into small dice

1 clove garlic, minced

1 sprig thyme

Salt and freshly ground black pepper

2 cups Chicken Stock (page 30)

1 bunch cavalo nero (sold as Tuscan kale or black kale) or any kale, stems trimmed and leaves cut into thick ribbons (chiffonade)

2 to 4 large eggs

○ Brush the sourdough bread with 2 tablespoons of the olive oil and grill both slices of bread on an outdoor grill or indoors on a cast-iron grill pan on the stove. Cut the bread into cubes and set aside.

○ Bring a pot of water to a boil and add the vinegar.

○ In a separate stockpot over high heat, add the remaining 2 tablespoons olive oil and decease the heat to medium. Add the bacon, onion, and carrot and cook, stirring every so often, until the onion starts to turn translucent, about 2 minutes. Add the garlic and thyme and season with salt and pepper. Add the stock and half of the grilled bread cubes and simmer for 5 minutes. In a blender, puree the soup or puree directly in the pot with an immersion blender. Return the soup to the pot and season to taste. Add the kale and simmer until just tender, 3 to 5 minutes.

○ Poach the eggs (see page 13) in the barely simmering pot of vinegar water.

○ To serve, ladle the soup into bowls and set a poached egg in each bowl. Garnish with some of the remaining grilled bread cubes.

French ONION SOUP with GOUGÈRES

With traditional French onion soup, you add a toasted bread crouton to the top of the soup plus some grated Gruyère cheese, broil it, and serve with another shot of sherry to pour on top or just drink. This is classic and I love it. But I also think that a few gougères, a Burgundian pastry puff hors d'oeuvre flavored with Gruyère, is a wonderful accompaniment to the soup and a fun twist—Gruyère in the pastry that goes with the soup rather than melted on the soup. Making choux pastry is definitely from my pastry chef repertoire, and I will guide you through making it. The results are well worth it and if you can make gougères, then you can make the choux pastry without cheese at another time, and stuff them with ice cream and finish with chocolate sauce to make profiteroles!

SERVES 2 TO 4

2 tablespoons olive oil

5 tablespoons unsalted butter

2 onions, halved and thinly sliced

2 cloves garlic, minced

1 teaspoon plus a pinch of sugar

4 cups Beef Stock (page 31) or Chicken Stock (page 30)

2 ounces sherry

$1/2$ teaspoon salt, plus more for seasoning

Freshly ground black pepper

$1/2$ cup whole milk

$1/2$ cup water

$1/2$ cup plus 2 tablespoons all-purpose flour

4 large eggs

$1/2$ cup grated Gruyère cheese

$1/4$ cup grated Parmesan cheese

Dash of Tabasco sauce

3 tablespoons minced fresh chives

○ Preheat the oven to 400°F.

○ For the soup, in a medium stockpot over high heat, add the olive oil and 1 tablespoon of the butter. Decrease the heat to low and add the onions, garlic, and pinch of sugar and cook until the onions start to caramelize, about 15 minutes. Add the stock and sherry, and season with a couple heavy pinches of salt and some pepper. Bring to a simmer and cook for another 20 minutes. Adjust the seasonings.

○ While the soup is cooking, make the choux pastry for the gougères. In a small saucepan, add the milk, water, the remaining 4 tablespoons butter, remaining 1 teaspoon sugar, and the $1/2$ teaspoon salt, and bring to a boil over high heat.

○ Turn off the heat and add the flour all at once. Whisk to incorporate. Turn the heat back on and with a wooden spoon, continue to stir and cook the mixture for another minute. Dump the choux into the bowl of a stand mixer fitted with the paddle attachment and add

(continued)

the eggs, 1 at a time, beating well on medium speed after each addition. Add the grated Gruyère and Parmesan cheeses (reserving about 1 tablespoon Parmesan), Tabasco, and chives.

○ Preheat the oven to 400°F. Line a baking sheet with parchment paper.

○ Fill a pastry bag fitted with a plain tip with the pastry. Or, using 2 spoons, scoop a large marble size of the dough onto the parchment paper. Pipe the pastry into large kisses on the parchment paper. Dip a finger in cold water and then lightly touch the top of each gougère to press down the tip. Sprinkle the gougères with the remaining 1 tablespoon grated Parmesan. At this point, you can freeze the balls and reserve to bake at any time.

○ Decrease the oven temperature to 375°F and bake until puffed and golden brown, about 20 minutes.

○ To serve, ladle the soup into bowls, put the soup bowl on a plate, and serve with the hot gougères, with or without a shot of sherry on the side.

SNACK **ATTACK** + COCKTAILS

ON THOSE intense days when hitting the pause button is just not an option for me, I want immediate gratification when I get home. I want a cocktail and some bar food, but not that frozen or greasy bar food or any junk food at all. It seems bizarre on some level that people can be nostalgic for the boxed macaroni and cheese of their childhood or yearn for a stack of Buffalo chicken wings from a long-ago game night, but we see updated versions of them on just about every bar menu these days, and they're wildly popular. I'm not saying to banish the fun factor from snacking or that fried chicken wings are healthy, but—I just want to make snacks better, using the best ingredients possible and with some exciting flavor combinations. Good fun food and drinks. That's what the recipes in this chapter are about. And here's a bonus: yes, this is the snack chapter, but team up a few of the dishes—as I often do—and you've got a great, light meal or some party-worthy hors d'oeuvres as well as some great cocktails to add to the festivities.

HOT WINGS, Three Ways

I played competitive amateur soccer for twenty-eight years and after a grueling soccer match, there's nothing better than ice-cold beers and a plate of uber-spicy, hot crispy fried chicken wings.

Working on the line in a restaurant can feel (and be) as brutal and exhausting as a soccer game, which is why most cooks do want to go out for beers after work and eat snacks that feed a hunger for food with a punch of heat to go with it.

The wings of chicken are great cuts of meat. There's just about the same amount of bone and meat, so they stay moist when cooked and don't need marinating. Deep-frying is the best way to cook wings because that hot heat from the frying oil seals in all that juciness and gives a crisp exterior. When they're done, just smother them in a flavor-packed sauce and enjoy with a tall, cold one. This recipe can easily be doubled or more.

SERVES 1 OR 2

CHICKEN WINGS

6 chicken wings

$1/2$ cup all-purpose flour

$1^1/2$ teaspoons salt

Freshly ground black pepper

2 cups canola oil, for frying

SAUCES

Habanero BBQ Syrup (page 16)

Chinese Black Bean–Sesame Sauce (page 76)

Moroccan Ginger Sauce (page 78)

○ Line a plate with paper towels and have ready. Cut off the very end tips of the chicken wings and discard. Cut the wings in half where the joint bones meet. Make sure the wings are dry. In a bowl, combine the flour, salt, and pepper; add the wing pieces and toss to coat. In a large cast-iron skillet or a small stockpot, heat the oil to 350°F on a deep-fat thermometer. Shake off any excess coating from the wings and drop the pieces into the hot oil. Cook for 6 to 8 minutes. With a slotted spoon, remove the wings from the pan to a bowl. Toss with $1/2$ cup of the sauce of your choice until evenly coated. Serve immediately.

(continued)

Habanero BBQ Syrup

¹/₂ cup Habenero BBQ Syrup (page 16)

○ Use ¹/₂ cup of the Habanero BBQ Syrup (page 16) as the sauce for the Chicken Wings Serve the syrup-coated wings hot and Buffalo style—with chilled celery sticks, some blue cheese dressing (from Tomato-Centric Cobb Salad, page 36), and an ice cold beer.

Chinese Black Bean–Sesame Sauce

It's a battle to decide which of these sauces for wings I like the most. I love the Chinese fermented black beans with ginger, garlic, and green onions. A little heat and a little sesame makes this addictive. It also goes well with an ice-cold beer.

MAKES ABOUT ¹/₂ CUP

1 teaspoon cornstarch

¹/₄ cup water

2 teaspoons canola oil

4 cloves garlic, minced

2 tablespoons grated fresh ginger

1 tablespoons fermented black beans or dark soy sauce

¹/₄ cup sliced green onions

2 tablespoons rice wine vinegar

1 tablespoon honey or molasses

1 teaspoon toasted sesame oil

¹/₄ teaspoon red pepper flakes (optional)

1 tablespoon toasted sesame seed

○ Combine the cornstarch and water in a small bowl and stir to make a slurry.

○ In a large sauté pan over medium heat, add the canola oil. Add the garlic, ginger, black beans, and green onions and sauté quickly for a couple of minutes. Add the water and cornstarch mixture, vinegar, and honey. Stir until the cornstarch starts to thicken the sauce, about a minute or two. Add the sesame oil and red pepper flakes.

○ Put ¹/₂ cup of the sauce in a bowl, add the hot fried wings, and toss until evenly coated. Serve hot, sprinkled with the sesame seeds.

(continued)

Moroccan Ginger Sauce

Jennifer Cox, a friend and former chef at Citizen Cake, opened her restaurant Montage in San Francisco years before working at Citizen Cake. She had an appetizer of Moroccan chicken wings on her menu that were so memorable. This sauce is inspired by them. Preserved lemons can be bought at specialty markets and at Whole Foods Markets. Alternatively, you can use some lemon zest.

MAKES ABOUT $1/2$ CUP

1 tablespoon olive oil

2 tablespoons minced garlic

2 tablespoons grated fresh ginger

$1/2$ cup freshly squeezed orange juice

$1/4$ cup water

2 tablespoons minced preserved lemon, or
    2 teaspoons Microplaned lemon zest

1 tablespoon honey

$1/2$ teaspoon orange blossom water

$1/2$ teaspoon ground cinnamon

$1/4$ teaspoon crushed coriander seed

1 teaspoon ground turmeric

$1/2$ teaspoon cayenne pepper

Salt and freshly ground black pepper

1 tablespoon minced fresh parsley, for garnish

1 tablespoon minced fresh cilantro, for
    garnish

$1/4$ cup dry-cured olives, for serving

$1/4$ cup roasted almonds, for serving

○ In a sauté pan over medium heat, add the olive oil. Add the garlic, ginger, orange juice, and water and bring to a simmer. Add the preserved lemon or lemon zest, honey, orange blossom water, cinnamon, coriander, turmeric, and cayenne pepper. Cook until the sauce is reduced a bit, another 3 to 4 minutes. Season with salt and pepper.

○ Put $1/2$ cup of the sauce in a bowl, add the hot fried wings, and toss until evenly coated. Serve hot, sprinkled with the parsley and cilantro, with the olives and almonds alongside.

Scrambled EGG CROSTINI with ASPARAGUS

If my dad had to cook dinner, once in a while he'd make us eggs and as a kid I thought it was weird to eat "breakfast" for dinner. I grew out of that, especially after becoming a chef. Whenever we cook for ourselves in a restaurant (the family meal), we eat daytime food, nighttime food—all different kinds of meals that don't necessarily match up to the meal clock of a normal person (that is, not a chef). I eat pasta for breakfast and I eat eggs for dinner. Scrambled eggs on crostini is an anytime snack for me. When you cook the eggs, remove them when they are about 75 percent done because they will continue to cook on the plate as they are cooling.

MAKES 10 CROSTINI, SERVES 2 AS AN HORS D'OEUVRE

$^1/_2$ baguette, cut on the diagonal (at a very sharp angle) into slices (about 10 slices)

2 tablespoons extra-virgin olive oil, plus more for drizzling

Salt and freshly ground black pepper

12 spears asparagus

$^1/_4$ teaspoon grated lemon zest (preferably from a Meyer lemon)

Squeeze of lemon juice (preferably from a Meyer lemon)

4 Scrambled Eggs (page 14)

○ Preheat the oven to 375°F. Drizzle the bread slices with olive oil. Sprinkle with salt and arrange on a baking sheet. Toast in the oven until golden, 15 to 20 minutes.

○ Prepare an ice bath (a bowl of ice water). Snap off the pale ends of the asparagus spears. With a vegetable peeler, peel 4 of the spears lengthwise into thin slices and reserve in the ice bath; they will curl as they sit in the water. Cut the remaining 8 spears on the diagonal into thin slices. In a saucepan of boiling water over high heat, blanch the asparagus pieces for 1 minute; drain.

○ Place the blanched asparagus in a bowl. Drain the chilled asparagus curls and add to the bowl. Add the remaining 2 tablespoons olive oil, lemon zest and juice, salt, and pepper, and toss.

○ To serve, divide the toasted bread between 2 plates. Spoon some scrambled eggs onto each crostini and top with the asparagus. Serve immediately.

HAM and BISCUIT SLIDERS with HOT PEPPER JAM

Chile jam is what makes these little biscuit sliders rock. I have made hot chile jams using all kinds of hot peppers, some milder, some hotter. You can use a prepared jam here—try a few to find the one you like best.

This is a rich little sandwich, a classic Southern combination that I could eat anytime. Also, the biscuits are pretty much good with anything you can imagine.

MAKES 12 BISCUITS

BISCUITS

2 cups all-purpose flour

$1/4$ cup sugar

1 tablespoon baking powder

$1/2$ teaspoon baking soda

2 teaspoons salt

4 ounces (1 stick) cold unsalted butter, plus 4 tablespoons at room temperature

$1/2$ cup grated white Cheddar cheese

$1/4$ cup buttermilk

$1/4$ cup heavy cream

1 large egg

2 tablespoons water

$1/2$ cup chile jam, for serving

$1/4$ cup thinly sliced ham

○ Combine the flour, sugar, baking powder, baking soda, and salt in a bowl. Work in the 4 ounces butter with your fingertips until the mixture is the texture of small beads. Toss in the grated cheese. Add the buttermilk and cream and work gently to combine but still keeping the texture shaggy. Wrap the dough in plastic wrap and refrigerate for at least 30 minutes.

○ Preheat the oven to 350°F. Line a baking sheet with parchment paper.

○ Remove the dough from the refrigerator. Lightly flour a surface. With a rolling pin, roll out the dough on the floured surface to an 8 by 12-inch rectangle; fold in half crosswise.

○ Add more flour to the work surface if necessary, and roll the dough out again to an 8 by 12-inch rectangle; fold in half crosswise. Roll out once again to an 8 by 12-inch rectangle. Using a sharp knife or biscuit cutter, cut into 3-inch squares or rounds. Set the biscuits on the prepared baking sheet.

○ Whisk the egg and the 2 tablespoons water together to make an egg wash, and brush the mixture on the biscuit tops. Bake until golden, 25 to 30 minutes. Cool slightly.

○ Slice each biscuit in half. Spread the biscuits with the 4 tablespoons butter and chile jam and fill with sliced ham. Serve warm or cool.

ANDOUILLE CORN Skillet CAKE

Here is a hangover cure or a potential hangover saver! Cornbread helps soak up your libations. This is just divine and absolutely necessary to eat late at night when you've had too much to drink or as a way to ease you into the next day. The spicy, smoky, salty andouille sausage combined with butter-slathered cornbread and cane syrup from Louisanna makes this Southern-inspired combination so addictive. You don't have to be drinking or be drunk to enjoy this. It's one of those savory and sweet dishes that is a hit every time.

SERVES 2 TO 4

2 cups cornmeal

1 cup all-purpose flour

$1/4$ cup sugar

2 teaspoons baking powder

$1^1/2$ teaspoons salt

$1/2$ teaspoon chipotle or ancho chile powder

A crank of black pepper

3 large eggs

1 cup buttermilk

$1/2$ cup canola oil

$1/2$ cup sautéed onion or green onions (optional)

4 tablespoons unsalted butter, plus more for serving

2 links andouille sausage, cut into 1-inch chunks

Cane syrup or molasses, for serving

○ Preheat the oven to 350°F.

○ For the cornbread, in a large bowl, combine the cornmeal, flour, sugar, baking powder, salt, chile powder, and black pepper. In a separate bowl, whisk together the eggs, buttermilk, and canola oil. Add the wet ingredients to the dry and stir just to combine. Add the sautéed onion.

○ Heat a large cast-iron skillet over high heat and add the butter to melt.

○ Remove from the heat and add the cornbread batter. Plug the sausage chunks throughout the cake while the batter is still raw. Set the skillet in the oven and bake for 25 to 30 minutes. Cornbread will spring back to the touch. Remove and cool slightly in the skillet.

○ Cut into wedges and serve warm with cane syrup or molasses and extra butter.

BABA GANOUSH

I have a thing for eggplant. After all, I have three recipes in this chapter that feature this versatile nightshade, which is actually a fruit (as is its nightshade relative, the tomato). And in each recipe, the eggplant tastes completely different. Baba ganoush, one of the most famous of eggplant dishes, is popular throughout the Middle East as a salad or side dish. Every culture and country has its own interpretation, using different spices or adding ingredients like mayonnaise or pomegranate concentrate. This is delicious with grilled flatbread (see pizza dough, page 98) or with pita bread, naan (the Indian flatbread), or crackers. Try it with a couple of tablespoons of Harissa (page 19) stirred in or along with it.

MAKES ABOUT 2 CUPS

1 large Italian eggplant (1 to 1¹/₄ pounds)

3 tablespoons olive oil

2 cloves garlic, chopped

2 tablespoons freshly squeezed lemon juice

1 tablespoon tahini (sesame seed paste)

1 teaspoon toasted and ground cumin seed or ground cumin

Salt and freshly ground black pepper

2 tablespoons minced fresh parsley leaves

○ Grill the whole eggplant on a hot grill or roast over a gas burner on medium heat on the stove top until charred and completely soft in the center, about 20 to 25 minutes. Cool for 10 minutes or more. Remove and discard the charred skin and remove the stem. Coarsely chop the meat and set aside in a bowl.

○ In a sauté pan over medium heat, add the olive oil and the garlic. Sauté the garlic for 30 seconds. Decrease the heat to medium-low, add the chopped eggplant and lemon juice, and cook for about 5 minutes.

○ Add the cooked eggplant to a food processor along with the tahini, ground cumin, and a large pinch of salt and pepper. Process and add more salt and pepper to taste. Stir in the parsley.

○ Cover and chill in the refrigerator for up to 3 days. Baba ganoush is best served at room temperature.

CAPONATA with BURRATA and GRILLED BREAD

One of my first jobs as a teenager was at The Italian Deli in Agoura Hills, California. I was smitten with the De Giosa family, the owners. They made absolutely everything there, including the bread, tomato sauce, all the salads, and the cannoli. Gina, the mama, made the caponata. I remember her standing over a large skillet at least once a week to make it. I loved this classic cold eggplant-based salad back then.

When I went to Rome with my mother in 2010, we had one of the best versions of caponata ever at lunch one day. It was served with an unbelievable smoked provolone. I've come to like a certain balance of sweet and savory in my caponata, so this is a combination of everything I know about balancing the flavors and textures of the roasted eggplant, peppers, raisins, and capers with the soft crunch of the toasted pine nuts. I have added chiles, because I like a little heat, but they can be left out and not missed here. If you have been hiding under a rock and do not know what burrata is, you need to run to your local Italian deli or to a supermarket and get some. Burrata is a hand-stretched fresh mozzarella-type cheese made with water buffalo milk and cream and is highly perishable, so you have to eat it as soon as you open it. It is indulgent and totally worth it.

SERVES 2 TO 4

1 medium eggplant, unpeeled, cut into
   $1/2$-inch cubes (about 3 cups cubes)

2 teaspoons salt

2 Fresno chiles or Calabrian canned chiles, chopped

4 tablespoons olive oil, plus more for drizzling

1 cup chopped red onion

4 cloves garlic, sliced

$1/2$ teaspoon dried oregano

1 cup chopped tomato

2 teaspoons tomato paste or ketchup

2 tablespoons raisins

1 tablespoon capers, rinsed

$1/4$ cup kalamata olives, pitted and chopped

$1/4$ cup loosely packed fresh basil leaves, torn

$1/2$ cup toasted pine nuts (see page 39)

Salt and freshly ground black pepper

2 thick slices ciabatta bread

1 or 2 balls burrata or fresh mozzarella cheese (about 8 ounces)

$1/4$ teaspoon *fleur de sel* (French sea salt)

○ Sweat the eggplant by placing the cubes in a bowl and tossing with the 2 teaspoons salt. Set aside for 5 minutes.

○ Roast the chiles directly over fire from a burner on the stove or on a grill to blister and blacken the skin. Remove from the heat and cover with plastic wrap or place in a closed container to steam the skin loose. Set aside.

○ Rub the eggplant cubes with a clean kitchen towel or paper towel to remove some of the moisture. Heat the 4 tablespoons olive oil in a 12-inch sauté pan over high heat. Add the eggplant to the pan and decrease the heat to medium. Cook the eggplant, tossing, for 1 minute. Add the chopped onion and cook for another 2 minutes. Decrease the heat to medium-low and add the garlic, oregano, tomato, tomato paste, and raisins and cook for another 2 minutes. Remove the skin from the chiles. Cut off the ends, split the chiles in half, and remove the seeds. Cut the chiles into small dice and add to the eggplant mixture. Turn off the heat. Add the capers, olives, basil, and toasted pine nuts. Adjust the seasoning with salt and pepper. Pour into a bowl and set aside.

○ Heat a grill or grill pan over high heat. Drizzle or brush olive oil on both sides of the bread and grill each side for about 45 seconds to 1 minute per side.

○ To serve, place the burrata on a large serving plate and sprinkle with the *fleur de sel*. Spoon a large amount, about 1 cup or more, of the caponata next to the burrata and serve with the grilled bread.

Strange-Flavored EGGPLANT

Barbara Tropp was an amazing pioneering woman chef in San Francisco whom I, and most everyone who knew her, just adored. Barbara opened a restaurant on Post Street in 1986 called China Moon, and people came from all over to experience Barbara's California-Chinese cuisine. The restaurant had a beautiful Art Deco style, the woks were used in the front window, and every table had a little crock of pickled ginger in syrup. The food was very memorable—full of flavor and style. As an eggplant lover, I have always cherished this BT (as many people, especially cooks, called her) recipe. It is delicious with steamed Chinese buns or just on crostini (see page 28), which is how she served it at China Moon. I have added fish sauce to the recipe, but it is optional.

MAKES 2 CUPS

1 large Italian eggplant (1 to 1$^{1}/_{4}$ pounds)

2 tablespoons canola oil

1 tablespoon minced garlic

1 tablespoon minced fresh ginger

$^{1}/_{4}$ cup sliced green onions (green and white parts)

$^{1}/_{2}$ teaspoon red pepper flakes

3 tablespoons soy sauce

3 tablespoons brown sugar

1 tablespoon Japanese rice wine vinegar

$^{1}/_{2}$ teaspoon Asian fish sauce (optional)

1 tablespoon hot water

$^{1}/_{2}$ teaspoon toasted sesame oil

Salt and freshly ground black pepper

○ Grill the whole eggplant over a medium-low flame until charred and completely soft in the center (see page 83). Cool for 10 minutes. Remove and discard the charred skin and remove the stem. Puree in a blender or chop into a mash and set aside in a bowl.

○ In a hot sauté pan or wok over high heat, add the oil and decrease the heat to medium. Add the garlic, ginger, green onions, and red pepper flakes and sauté for about 15 seconds. Add the soy sauce, brown sugar, vinegar, fish sauce, the 1 tablespoon hot water, the sesame oil, and the eggplant puree. Stir to blend and remove from the heat. Season to taste with salt and pepper.

OYSTERS in the Fire

I have a T-shirt someone gave me that says "Oystergirl" on the front, and that's just what I am—an oyster girl! I love oysters from both the East and the West coasts.

Forty-nine miles north of San Francisco you can enjoy fresh oysters harvested from Tomales Bay at Hog Island Oyster Farm. You can buy, grill, and eat them right there on the bay, and lots of people do just that. This area in Northern California is absolutely one of the most beautiful and magical places in the world. I think the Kumamotos from Hog Island are best raw. Similarly, East Coast oysters such as Wellfleets or other Masssachusettes oysters are great raw because of their extra brininess. But the bigger, meatier, and creamier ones from either coast are good grilled or just set on a sheet pan in a wood-burning oven or fireplace. All I really want on these is melted butter, Tabasco, and a few drops of lime juice. The Roasted Tomato–Chipotle Salsa (page 23) is a great alternative accompaniment on raw, grilled, or roasted oysters.

SERVES 2 TO 4

24 fresh oysters in the shell
4 tablespoons unsalted butter, melted

1 teaspoon Tabasco sauce
1 lime, quartered

○ Place the oysters on a preheated grill rack or on a baking sheet set over a fire and allow them to open (from the pressure of the steam that builds up inside the oyster as it heats up), about 3 to 5 minutes, depending on the heat of the fire.

○ Meanwhile, melt the butter in a small saucepan and add the Tabasco.

○ To serve, set the opened oysters on a serving plate. Drizzle each oyster with Tabasco butter sauce and a squeeze of lime juice. Serve immediately.

Violet GIN FIZZ

A gin fizz is a lovely, effervescent cocktail for brunch and this one with violet, is a beautiful way to start off a slow moving day. It's like a grown up egg cream with floral notes.

MAKES 1 DRINK

2 ounces gin

1 ounce fresh lemon juice

1 egg white

2 teaspoons Crème de Violette

$1/2$ ounce heavy cream

2 drops orange blossom water

Splash of club soda

Violet flowers for garnish

○ Combine gin, lemon juice, egg white, Crème de Violette, heavy cream, and orange blossom water in a cocktail shaker and add ice. Shake vigorously until you can hear that the ice has shattered. Strain into a glass and finish off with a splash of club soda.

○ Garnish with violet petals

Pomegranate PISCO SOUR

Pisco is a nice change of pace for a spirit and there are many flavors of pisco. I use a Peruvian aromatic variety. Pomegranate juice makes this a gorgeous cocktail.

MAKES 1 DRINK

2 ounces Pisco

1 ounce pomegranate juice

½ ounce lime juice

1 teaspoon sugar

1 egg white

Dash of Angostura bitters

○ Combine pisco, pomegranate juice, lime juice, sugar, and egg white in a cocktail shaker with ice and shake vigorously until you can hear that the ice has shattered. Strain into a chilled glass and garnish with a dash of bitters.

NYE in ITALY

I came up with this festive cocktail one year while catering a small party on New Year's Eve. The Campari, a classic Italian aperitif, gives it a great color and the extra bitterness.

MAKES 2 DRINKS

2 ounces gin

4 ounces fresh tangerine juice

1 ounce Campari

Splash of Prosecco

Tangerine peel, for garnish

○ Combine gin, tangerine juice, and Campari in a cocktail shaker with ice and shake steadily for about twenty shakes. Strain over ice into two glasses and top with a splash of Prosecco and finish with a twist of tangerine peel.

P&B (Pig and Booze)

The pig and boozed themed dinners we did at Orson are all great memories. One of the last ones we did was "Beast, Booze & Backs" and this cocktail is based on that.

Try it with anything pork!

MAKES 1 DRINK

2 oz. bourbon, such as Bulleit

1 oz. Canton ginger liqueur

$1/2$ ounce pickle brine

1 ounce root beer

Lemon twist, for garnish

○ Stir together bourbon, ginger liqueur and pickle brine with ice, (preferably a large ice cube) and top with root beer. Finish with a twist of lemon.

NEGRONI

I'm not changing a thing about the classic. It is traditional to serve this up, but I prefer it with one large ice cube.

MAKES 1 DRINK

1 ounce Plymoth Gin

1 ounce Punt e Mes

1 ounce Campari

Orange twist, for garnish

○ Pour gin, Punt e Mes, and Campari over ice in a shaker and shake vigorously until ice has shattered. Strain and serve up with a twist of orange. Alternatively, combine the gin, Punt e Mes and Campari with ice and stir. Strain over a large ice cube in a rocks glass and garnish with a twist of orange.

PIZZA, GIRL MEETS GRILL

I LOVE PIZZA more and more. I've got a friend in San Francisco, Tony Gemignani, who makes so many varieties, from different Italian styles to all kinds of East Coast styles. At his restaurant, Tony's Pizza Napoletana, in San Francisco's North Beach, he has four different kinds of pizza ovens: a wood-burning stove much like I have at my restaurant, a coal burning oven, a deck, and a rotating brick oven. And I know he is always thinking of more ways to cook one of the world's favorite dishes. If I am not making pizza at home, and I am hungry for it, then I am usually at his place.

Baking pizza at home is challenging. Most home ovens don't get hot enough to bake the dough fast enough. Pizza baked in a home oven is doughier, and more like focaccia. Pizza stones are an interesting idea and I have used them and they will help with a crisp crust, but I prefer the high heat of the grill because I can get the char on the dough and that blistering on the crust fast. I have a propane-fueled outdoor grill that works great for this purpose. After I grill the pizza on both sides, I move the dough onto a pizza paddle or the back of a sheet pan dusted with a little semolina flour. Then I set a large cast-iron pizza griddle on my outdoor grill on the grates, close the top, and let it get really hot. I add the toppings and then slide the pizza onto the griddle and let it bake for about 10 minutes, or until the cheese is melted and the crust is getting crisp and brown. If you have a charcoal grill, wait until the coals are starting to gray (just as you would cook anything on this type of fire). If you have an indoor grill on your stove or have a stove-top griddle, set it on medium-high heat and let it get hot before grilling the dough on both sides, then move the dough to a sheet pan to put toppings on and finish cooking the pizza in an oven preheated to 500°F for about 10 minutes, or until the cheese is melted and the dough is crisp and brown.

PIZZA DOUGH

MAKES ONE 12-INCH PIZZA CRUST

3 cups (14 ounces) unbleached white flour

1 teaspoon active dry yeast

1 cup warm water (105°F to 115°F)

1 tablespoon salt

1 tablespoon olive oil

○ Add the flour to a large mixing bowl or to the bowl of a stand mixer fitted with the dough hook. In a separate bowl, combine the yeast with the warm water and stir together. Set aside for 1 to 2 minutes. When the yeast mixture starts to bubble after a couple of minutes, it is ready to use. Add the yeast to the flour and start to mix together.

○ If making by hand, dump the mixture onto a counter lightly dusted with flour and knead for 5 to 6 minutes. Add the salt and knead for another 2 minutes, and add a little more flour if necessary to form an elastic dough. If making in the stand mixer, knead on low for 5 to 6 minutes, until the dough starts to become smooth and elastic. Add the salt and knead for another 2 minutes. In a large clean bowl, add the olive oil. Form the dough into a ball, put in the bowl, and turn the dough around until it is entirely coated with oil. Cover the bowl with plastic wrap and refrigerate for 12 hours. It will double in bulk and start to develop a yeasty aroma.

○ The dough is now ready to use, but for a more flavorful dough, punch it down and reform into a tight ball. Put the dough ball back in the bowl, cover, and refrigerate for another 12 hours.

○ To grill the dough, preheat the grill on high. Slide the dough onto the hot grill and cook until grill marks appear and the dough is set, about 2 minutes. Carefully flip the dough over with a large spatula or tongs or your hands; brush the top with olive oil, and cook until the dough is firm but not completely cooked and grill marks appear, another 3 to 4 minutes. Slip the pizza paddle under the crust and remove from the grill. Set a large cast-iron griddle on the grill to heat or place a pizza pan in the oven and preheat to 500°F.

Margarita PIZZA

This is my go-to pizza. I don't need a lot of bells and whistles, but I need the best of the best ingredients on this kind of pie. A good dough, a great sauce, fresh mozzarella, and basil are really where it's at.

MAKES ONE 12- TO 13-INCH PIZZA

2 tablespoons flour, for the work surface

1 ball Pizza Dough (page 98)

1 tablespoon semolina flour, for the pizza paddle

2 tablespoons olive oil, for brushing the dough

$1/2$ cup Tomato Sauce (page 26)

8 ounces fresh mozzarella cheese, drained and cut into 6 chunks (not slices)

$1/4$ cup grated pecorino romano cheese

Salt and freshly ground black pepper

8 Genovese basil leaves (see Note, following)

Extra-virgin olive oil, for drizzling

○ Preheat the grill on high heat.

○ Dust a counter with the 2 tablespoons flour. Stretch the dough by rotating on your knuckles into a 12- to 13-inch diameter round. Sprinkle the semolina on a wooden pizza paddle or on the back of a baking pan large enough to hold the dough round. Set the dough on the semolina. Brush the top of the dough with the olive oil.

○ Slide the pizza onto the hot grill and cook until grill marks appear and the dough is set, about 2 minutes. Carefully flip the dough over with a large spatula or tongs or your hands; brush the top with olive oil, and cook until the dough is firm but not completely cooked and grill marks appear, another 3 to 4 minutes. Slip the pizza paddle under the crust and remove from the grill. Set a large cast-iron griddle on the grill to heat or place a pizza pan in the oven and preheat to 500°F.

○ To build the pizza, spread the tomato sauce over the partially cooked crust. Distribute the mozzarella over the pizza and sprinkle on the pecorino romano. Season with salt and pepper.

○ Slip the pizza off the paddle onto the griddle on the grill or onto the pizza pan in the oven and bake until bubbly, 15 to 20 minutes. Remove and set the pizza on a cutting board. Scatter on whole or snipped basil leaves and drizzle with the extra-virgin olive oil. Cut into 6 to 8 wedges and serve.

Note: Genovese basil is the most common variety in our grocery stores. As alternatives, look for these other basil varieties (or grow them yourself) that are favorites of mine: Greek basil has very small leaves and little bursts of concentrated basil flavor; opal basil has purple leaves that look gorgeous on pizza, with more licorice notes; lemon basil blends the flavor of basil with lemon balm in a very delicious way.

Spanish PIZZA

This pizza is about some of my favorite flavors from Spain. In California in late summer, farmers' markets offer small sweet piquillo peppers, which I roast over an open fire, sweat to loosen their skins, then peel. But I also love them right from a can or jar. Either fresh or prepared can be used here. Spanish chorizo is a hard, cured salami with smoked paprika in the spice mixture, unlike Mexican chorizo, which is made from fresh pork and is soft. It will remind you a little of pepperoni. I finish the pizza with olives and Manchego cheese, both of which are salty so I don't think any extra seasoning is needed beyond what's called for in the recipe.

MAKES ONE 12- TO 13-INCH PIZZA

2 tablespoons all-purpose flour, for the work surface

1 ball Pizza Dough (page 98)

1 tablespoon semolina flour, for the pizza paddle

2 tablespoons olive oil, for brushing

$^1/_2$ cup Tomato Sauce (page 26)

About 3 roasted, peeled piquillo peppers (from a jar or canned), cut into slivers

4 ounces fresh mozzarella, cut into chunks

20 thin slices Spanish chorizo (about 6 ounces)

2 tablespoons chopped olives (I like the dry-cured black olives)

$^1/_4$ cup shaved Manchego cheese (about 2 ounces)

Extra-virgin olive oil, for drizzling.

○ Preheat the grill on high.

○ Dust a counter with the 2 tablespoons flour. Stretch the dough by rotating on your knuckles into a 12- to 13-inch diameter round. Sprinkle the semolina on a wooden pizza paddle or on the back of a baking pan large enough to hold the dough round. Set the dough on the semolina. Brush the top of the dough with the olive oil.

○ Slide the pizza onto the hot grill and cook until grill marks appear and the dough is set, about 2 minutes. Carefully flip the dough over; brush the top with olive oil, and cook until the dough is firm but not completely cooked and grill marks appear, another 3 to 4 minutes. Slip the pizza paddle under the crust and remove from the grill. Set a large cast-iron griddle on the grill to heat or have a pizza pan in the oven and preheat to 500°F.

○ To build the pizza, spread the tomato sauce over the partially cooked crust, then distribute the slivered peppers, the slices of mozzarella, and the chorizo. Slip the pizza off the paddle onto the griddle on the grill or onto the pizza pan in the oven. Bake until bubbly, 15 to 20 minutes. Immediately scatter the olives and Manchego cheese over the pizza.

○ Remove from the heat and set the pizza on a cutting board. Drizzle with the extra-virgin olive oil, cut into 6 to 8 wedges, and serve immediately.

Pastrami PIZZA

I know pizza purists might think . . . pastrami?! But seriously, it seemed so right to my cooks and me at Orson one night. We make our own pastrami, and a killer pastrami sandwich was on our lunch menu. It just made sense that pastrami and everything that would go on a classic Reuben sandwich—Russian dressing, sauerkraut, Swiss cheese— would work on a crusty, chewy, grilled pizza crust. The best part was that none of us had made Russian dressing before. When I discovered it is syrup based, almost a gastrique (a vinegar-based sugar syrup), I realized it is the salty-sweetness of a Reuben that makes it so addictive, as well as its flavor-texture-crunch appeal. This pizza is perfect for grilling and finishing in the oven and really does transform the classic sandwich into a crazy cool pizza. I like the crunchiness of the quick sauerkraut, but you can also substitute a prepared sauerkraut. You have to try this!

MAKES ONE 12- TO 13-INCH PIZZA

RUSSIAN DRESSING

1/4 cup sugar

3 tablespoons water

1 shallot, minced

2 tablespoons ketchup

1 teaspoon Worcestershire sauce

1/2 teaspoon paprika (not smoked)

1/8 teaspoon celery seed

Juice of 1 lemon

1 teaspoon white wine vinegar

1/2 cup canola oil

Salt and freshly ground black pepper

PIZZA

1 cup shredded cabbage

1 teaspoon salt, plus more for seasoning

1/4 teaspoon caraway seed

2 tablespoons all-purpose flour, for the work surface

1 ball Pizza Dough (page 98)

1 tablespoon semolina flour, for the pizza paddle

2 tablespoons olive oil, for brushing

2 teaspoons Dijon mustard

1 cup grated Swiss cheese

2 tablespoons grated Parmesan cheese

10 thin slices pastrami (about 6 ounces)

○ For the dressing, in a saucepan, combine the sugar and the 3 tablespoons water and bring to a boil over medium heat. Whisk in the shallot, ketchup, Worcestershire, paprika, celery seed, lemon juice, and vinegar and bring back to a simmer. Slowly whisk in the canola oil and season with salt and pepper; remove from the heat and cool. The dressing can keep, stored in an airtight container, for 1 month in the refrigerator.

○ For the pizza, toss the shredded cabbage with the 1 teaspoon salt and caraway seed and let stand for 30 minutes at room temperature or overnight in the refrigerator.

(continued)

○ Preheat the grill on high.

○ Dust a counter with the 2 tablespoons flour. Stretch the dough by rotating on your knuckles into a 12- to 13-inch diameter round. Sprinkle the semolina on a wooden pizza paddle or on the back of a baking pan large enough to hold the dough round. Set the dough on the semolina. Brush the top of the dough with the olive oil.

○ Slide the pizza onto the hot grill and cook until grill marks appear and the dough is set, about 2 minutes. Carefully flip the dough over; drizzle or brush the top with olive oil, and cook until the dough is firm but not completely cooked and grill marks appear, another 3 to 4 minutes. Slip the pizza paddle under the crust and remove from the grill. Set a large cast-iron griddle on the grill to heat or have a pizza pan in the oven and preheat to 500°F.

○ To build the pizza, pour off any water that has drained form the cabbage. Toss the cabbage with the mustard and spread over the partially cooked crust. Sprinkle on the Swiss and Parmesan cheeses, season with salt and pepper, and pile on the pastrami. Slip the pizza off the paddle onto the griddle on the grill or onto the pizza pan in the oven and bake for about 10 minutes.

○ Remove from the heat and set the pizza on a cutting board. Drizzle with the Russian dressing, cut into 6 to 8 wedges, and serve immediately.

SAUSAGE and FENNEL PIZZA

I see and smell the wild fennel that grows throughout the Bay Area. I usually get strong whiffs of it in the springtime and in the late summer. I noticed one summer afternoon as I was driving around San Francisco how all the fennel was blooming with bright mustard-yellow flowers. I snipped off several tops of these plants and brought them to the restaurant to air-dry for a day. Then we picked off all the miniature flowers that carry the fennel pollen and it was so fragrant, I added the pollen to pizzas, pastas, chicken, salads, and so on. As a substitute, toast some fennel seed for 1 minute in a hot dry skillet and then grind in a spice grinder or with a mortar and pestle.

This pizza is completely inspired by Nancy Silverton's fennel and sausage pizza at Pizzaria Mozza in Los Angeles.

MAKES ONE 12- TO 13-INCH PIZZA

2 tablespoons all-purpose flour, for the work surface

1 ball Pizza Dough (page 98)

1 tablespoon semolina flour, for the pizza paddle

2 tablespoons olive oil, for brushing

$^1/_2$ cup Tomato Sauce (page 26)

$^1/_4$ cup thinly sliced red onion

$^1/_4$ cup thinly sliced fennel bulb

6 ounces bulk sweet Italian sausage

4 ounces ricotta cheese

2 tablespoons grated Parmesan cheese

$^1/_4$ teaspoon fennel pollen

○ Preheat the grill on high.

○ Dust your counter with the 2 tablespoons flour. Stretch the dough by rotating on your knuckles into a 12- to 13-inch diameter round. Sprinkle the semolina on a wooden pizza paddle or on the back of a baking pan large enough to hold the dough round. Set the dough on the semolina. Brush the top of the dough with the olive oil.

○ Slide the pizza onto the hot grill and cook until grill marks appear and the dough is set, about 2 minutes. Carefully flip the dough over; brush the top with the olive oil, and cook until the dough is firm but not completely cooked and grill marks appear, another 3 to 4 minutes. Slip the pizza paddle under the crust and remove from the grill. Set a large cast-iron griddle on the grill to heat or have a pizza pan in the oven and preheat to 500°F.

○ To build the pizza, spread the tomato sauce over the partially cooked crust, then distribute the onion and fennel over the sauce. Add the Italian sausage in chunks, then drop the ricotta in 6 to 8 large spoonfuls around the pizza. Sprinkle with the Parmesan. Slip the pizza off the paddle onto the griddle on the grill or onto the pizza pan in the oven. Bake until bubbly and the sausage is cooked through and browned, 15 to 20 minutes.

○ Remove from the heat and set the pizza on a cutting board. Sprinkle with the fennel pollen, cut into 6 to 8 wedges, and serve immediately.

EGG, MUSHROOM, and TRUFFLE PIZZA

This is a great pizza for any meal, and a bit luxurious, especially if you make it with chanterelle, porcini, or black trumpet mushrooms—or a mixture. With an egg, ricotta, a a bit of truffle oil, a sprinkle of hazelnuts, and a handful of arugula—it's a salad and main course all in one.

MAKES ONE 12- TO 13-INCH PIZZA

3 tablespoons olive oil

2 cups sliced mushrooms of any variety or a mixture (about 5 ounces)

1 shallot, minced

1 sprig thyme

Salt and freshly ground black pepper

4 ounces ricotta cheese

2 teaspoons truffle oil

1/2 teaspoon grated lemon zest

2 tablespoons all-purpose or bread flour, for the work surface

1 ball Pizza Dough (page 98)

1 tablespoon semolina flour, for the pizza paddle

1/4 cup grated Parmesan cheese

1/4 cup crushed hazelnuts (optional)

1 large egg

1 cup arugula (preferably wild)

Extra-virgin olive oil, for drizzling

Squeeze of lemon juice, for finishing

○ In a sauté pan, on high heat, add 1 tablespoon of the olive oil, then sauté the mushrooms for 2 minutes. Add the shallot and thyme, season with salt and pepper, and cook another 2 minutes. Cool and remove the thyme sprig. Mix the ricotta with the truffle oil and lemon zest and set aside.

○ Preheat the grill on high heat.

○ Dust a counter with the 2 tablespoons flour. Stretch the dough by rotating on your knuckles into a 12- to 13-inch diameter round. Sprinkle the semolina on a wooden pizza paddle or on the back of a baking pan large enough to hold the dough round. Set the dough on the semolina. Brush the top of the dough with some of the remaining olive oil.

○ Slide the pizza onto the hot grill and cook until grill marks appear and the dough is set, about 2 minutes. Carefully flip the dough over; brush the top with the remaining olive oil, and cook until the dough is firm but not completely cooked (not brown and crispy) and grill marks appear, another 3 to 4 minutes. Slip the pizza paddle under the crust and remove from the grill. Set a large cast-iron griddle on the grill to heat or place a pizza pan in the oven and preheat to 400°F.

○ To build the pizza, spread the cooked mushrooms on the partially cooked crust. Distribute the ricotta mixture in 4 big spoonfuls on the pizza. Sprinkle on the Parmesan cheese, then spread on the hazelnuts. Crack an egg in the center and season with salt and pepper. Slip the pizza off the paddle onto the griddle on the grill or onto the pizza pan in the oven and bake until the egg white is set, but the yolk is still runny in the middle, 12 to 15 minutes. Top with the arugula.

○ Remove from the heat and set the pizza on a cutting board. Drizzle with the extra-virgin olive oil and a squeeze of lemon, cut into 6 to 8 pieces, and serve immediately.

CONTAINS STARCH: PASTA, NOODLES, GRAINS, AND RICE

MY LIFE FOLLOWS the same frantic pace as the soundtrack to *Run Lola Run*, a 1998 German film about a punky redhead, Lola, who is running against time to survive and beat the odds. I sprint, lift, sweat, race, stress, cook, and direct all day and night. I am always racing against a clock or a deadline. I long for moments that hit my soul. I desire poetry to occur more often that it does. Living life as a chef at a relatively insane pace, I believe this is why I first of all need food that restores my body on a biological level, as well as feeds my soul. Pastas, grains, and rice—starchy foods—are the comfort foods that do this for me. I am rarely too tired to make my own pasta, and when I do, I make enough for a week and keep it in the freezer. Some of these dishes really don't take much time. My mom's noodles are really easy to make, and this dish is ultimate comfort food. Quinoa, black rice, and crab pad Thai sound pretty exotic and hopefully they are still approachable. These are some dishes that require a little ingredient gathering, but ultimately bring a lot of flavor and creativity to the comfort zone.

Homemade PASTA

Making your own pasta takes a little work, but it requires little time to cook, and the results are delicious. Like most doughs, this one is affected by weather and humidity, which can change the amount of liquid needed. If the dough feels really dry, add a few drops of water. It is better for the dough to be on the drier side since the liquid in the eggs will saturate the starch of the flour and the dough will eventually feel moist. You will need a pasta machine to roll out the dough.

MAKES APPROXIMATELY 1 POUND

20 ounces all-purpose or Italian "00" flour
(see Note, following)

1 teaspoon salt

4 large eggs

Semolina or rice flour, for dusting the dough

○ To make by hand, combine the flour and salt on a work surface and shape into a mound. Make a well in the center and crack the eggs into it. With a fork, draw the flour into the center of the mound to combine with the eggs and continue to mix with your hands until all the flour is incorporated.

○ Dust the surface with a little more flour, if necessary. Knead until the dough is firm, about 5 minutes. The dough will be dry and the flour will soak up the water as it rests. Cover with plastic wrap and rest at room temperature for about 30 minutes to 1 hour.

○ Dust lightly with flour and run through a pasta machine, starting at setting 1 and going to 5 or 6 if using a hand-crank "Atlas"-type machine. Cut into the desired shape. I stop at setting 5 and run through the spaghetti attachment for spaghetti and I also make hand-cut or hand-shaped pasta at this thickness. I go to setting 6 for ravioli or paparadelle. After I cut the pasta, I dust it heavily with semolina and let it rest at room temperature for an hour. Then I portion and set in plastic bags and freeze for later use.

Note: I like the "00" flour for pasta and pizza doughs. This is a stronger flour that will give the dough a better mouthfeel in the end, but all-purpose flour will work, too.

Contains Starch: Pasta, Noodles, Grains, and Rice

SPAGHETTI and MEATBALLS

Making great dumplings of all kinds is an art that I work hard to master. And meatballs are, after all, little dumplings. You want to keep meatballs light, not overworking them into tough little meat rocks. I like them medium size, and usually serve two per person on top of spaghetti with a spicy tomato sauce. My mix is two parts beef to one part pork when I make them for spaghetti. The beef is for the meaty flavor and the pork for the extra suave texture, plus it adds to the overall flavor. Some people like to sear meatballs or bake them before adding to a dish, but I prefer poaching them in stock. I think this gives them a softer texture and an even cooking time and when coated with tomato sauce, they are just delicious.

I make other types of meatballs with ground chicken and pork, or all chicken, or all lamb. For chicken meatballs, add a little chopped green onion, grated fresh ginger, and curry powder. For lamb meatballs, mix in ground cumin, ground sumac, and minced fresh parsley and mint. If making either of these two, I wouldn't serve them with grated cheese. Rather, I like chicken meatballs on a sandwich with cucumbers, yogurt, and cilantro. With lamb meatballs, I serve cooked chickpeas and Harissa (page 19) mixed in with the tomato sauce and olives, plus a drizzle of yogurt and some parsley leaves.

SERVES 4

MEATBALLS

2 tablespoons ground crackers or dried unseasoned bread crumbs, (**Note:** Panko and matzo meal work great for meatballs.)

2 tablespoons whole milk

8 ounces ground beef

4 ounces ground pork

1/2 teaspoon dried oregano

2 teaspoons grated pecorino romano

1/2 teaspoon garlic powder

1/2 teaspoon salt, plus more as needed

Freshly ground black pepper

1 large egg

2 cups Chicken Stock (page 30), Beef Stock (page 31), or purchased broth

SPAGHETTI

1 tablespoon salt, plus more for seasoning

1 pound Homemade Pasta (page 113) or 12 ounces dried spaghetti

1 1/2 cups Tomato Sauce (page 26)

Freshly ground black pepper

1/4 cup grated pecorino romano or Parmigiano-Reggiano cheese, for sprinkling

8 fresh basil leaves, torn, for garnish

○ For the meatballs, in a small bowl, combine the crackers with the milk and stir together. Set aside for 5 minutes.

(continued)

○ In a medium bowl, combine the ground beef, ground pork, oregano, grated pecorino, garlic powder, the $1/2$ teaspoon salt, pepper, and the egg. Add the cracker-milk mixture and gently knead together by hand quickly while keeping cold. Meaning, don't stand there playing with it for 5 minutes warming it up, because you will mess it up. It is important when making meatballs or sausage that the fat does not start to warm up (same with butter in a pie dough). If it stays cold, it will make a better emulsification and the fat will keep it nice and juicy. You can chill the meat before you make meatballs if it seems warm or if you are working in a warm environment.

○ Line a baking sheet or plate with parchment paper. Shape the meat mixture into balls that resemble oversize golf balls, set on the prepared baking sheet or plate, and refrigerate for 15 minutes. Add the stock to a medium saucepot and bring to a boil over high heat, then decrease the heat to a simmer. Drop in the meatballs and simmer, covered, for 20 minutes. Remove from heat.

○ For the spaghetti, bring a large pot filled with water to a boil over high heat and add the 1 tablespoon salt. Drop in the pasta and cook for 4 minutes if using fresh pasta, or 8 minutes if using dried pasta.

○ In a sauté pan over medium heat, add the sauce and 2 or 3 tablespoons of the pasta cooking water. Bring to a simmer and add the cooked pasta and the meatballs. Coat the pasta and the meatballs with the tomato sauce and simmer briefly to heat up. Season with salt and freshly ground black pepper.

○ To serve, divide among plates or bowls, sprinkle with the cheese, and garnish with the torn basil leaves.

SPAGHETTINI with CHERRY TOMATOES and MOZZARELLA

When I was in college in Southern California, I met Georgia, from Genoa, Italy, who was in one of my painting classes. She and her brother Giovanni invited me to their house in Beverly Hills and showed me how to make this very simple and delicious pasta dish. It is really about the ingredients. Spaghettini is one cut of pasta that I do not make fresh, because the cut is so thin, so I buy it dried, preferably by Barilla. I love dry-farmed tomatoes or cherry tomatoes from Dirty Girl Farms in California. The tomato flavor is more concentrated and bursts in this dish. Also, I love the extra-virgin olive oil from DeVero or McEvoy, both made from olives grown in orchards north of San Francisco. But any olive oil that's grassy green and a little spicy will work. This is a summer pasta for sure, but if you happen to can tomatoes or can get some good canned cherry tomatoes, use them.

SERVES 2

2 cups cherry tomatoes, halved

4 cloves garlic, minced or sliced

1 tablespoon kosher salt, plus more as needed

6 ounces dried spaghettini or capellini

$1/4$ cup extra-virgin olive oil

Freshly ground black pepper

4 ounces fresh mozzarella, cut into 1-inch chunks

2 teaspoons fresh oregano leaves

4 fresh basil leaves, torn

○ Put the tomato halves in a bowl with the garlic and season with salt.

○ For the spaghettini, bring a large pot filled with water to a boil over high heat and add the 1 tablespoon salt. Drop in the pasta and cook for 3 to 4 minutes. Drain and add to the bowl with the tomatoes. Add the olive oil, a few cranks of pepper, the mozzarella, and the oregano.

○ To serve, toss, divide between bowls, and garnish with the torn basil leaves.

Contains Starch: Pasta, Noodles, Grains, and Rice

GNOCCHI with WALNUT-BASIL PESTO

Gnocchi is so simple but a little tricky at the same time. Too little flour, and the dumplings break up in the water; too much flour, and they are tough. A great tip is to let the potatoes cool after they have been baked and grated through a ricer or food mill. Adding the flour to the steaming hot potatoes can create a gluey mixture. Keep gnocchi simple with a classic Italian sauce such as Walnut-Basil Pesto (page 27) or Tomato Sauce (page 26) or even just tossed in brown butter (see page 17) and lemon juice and finished with grated Parmesan cheese.

SERVES 2 TO 4

3 large russet potatoes

1/2 cup all-purpose flour, plus more for cutting

2 teaspoons salt

1 large egg

3/4 cup (6 ounces) Walnut-Basil Pesto (page 27)

4 tablespoons grated Parmesan cheese

○ Preheat the oven to 400°F. Wash and puncture the potatoes with a small paring knife or a fork in a few spots around the potatoes. Bake for 40 minutes, peel while hot, and then process through a food mill or ricer onto a sheet pan and let cool completely. Don't scoop up or move it around; just let the riced potato cool. Sprinkle the flour and salt over the potatoes and bring together to form into a mound. Make a well in the center of the mound and add the egg. Knead the dough gently until it comes together and forms a ball. Do not overwork. Roll the dough into a log on a lightly floured surface. Using a knife, cut the dough in half and then each in half again. Roll each piece of dough into a 1-inch-thick log. Cut into 3-inch pieces and roll each piece into a ball. Using a gnocchi board, roll the balls lightly across the board to form the gnocchi shape or just leave in balls. Place the formed gnocchi on a well-floured tray and refrigerate until ready to use. Gnocchi freezes well and should be frozen on the tray before putting in plastic bags or in an airtight container. When cooking gnocchi from the freezer, they can be taken directly from the freezer to boiling water.

○ Bring a large pot of salted water to a boil over high heat. Turn the heat down to medium-high. Drop the gnocchi into the boiling salted water and cook for about 3 to 4 minutes. They will float to the top of the water. Strain and rinse under cold water.

○ In a sauté pan over medium-high heat, add the pesto and the gnocchi. Sauté gently for just 2 to 3 minutes.

○ Divide among warm bowls and finish with some grated Parmesan cheese. Serve immediately.

CARBONARA

I finally went to Rome in 2010, traveling there with my mom. I wanted to go to the heart of some of the classic Roman dishes and I found exactly that. We met up with my friend Barbara Lynch, who is the chef at No. 9 Park, Sportello, and several other restaurants in Boston. Barbara knows a lot about pasta and is one of my favorite chefs. She and her friend Annie Copps, who I think may be the funniest person I have ever met, were just coming off a cooking marathon on a ship. They suggested we meet for lunch at Perilli, a trattoria in the Testaccio district, and we all had a religious experience with the pasta carbonara at this place. It was one of those times as a chef, when you think, well, what the hell have I been making or eating around the world that pretends to be carbonara? It was absolute perfection of egg yolk, pecorino, and pancetta poised with perfectly cooked rigatoni, a pasta I'd never had before with carbonara.

I am positive that this is still a Californication of the dish, but I wanted to share my experience and education. Please do not substitute bacon for the pancetta—it would add a smokiness that just doesn't belong in this dish. Also, this just works better with fresh rigatoni pasta if you can find it, but use dried if you can't.

SERVES 2

4 ounces pancetta, cut into $1/2$-inch pieces that are $1/8$ inch thick

Olive oil

1 tablespoon salt, plus more for seasoning

8 ounces fresh or dried rigatoni pasta

4 large egg yolks (from as fresh, free-range, and carotene-eating chickens that you can find)

Freshly ground black pepper

$1/4$ cup grated pecorino romano cheese

○ In a large sauté pan over low heat, add the pancetta and a splash of olive oil. Cook until the fat is rendered and the meat is just beginning to brown and crisp lightly, about 10 minutes; set aside.

○ For the pasta, bring a large pot filled with water to a boil over high heat and add the 1 tablespoon salt. Drop in the pasta and cook for 4 minutes if using fresh pasta, or 10 to 12 minutes if using dried pasta.

○ In a small bowl, whisk the egg yolks with 2 tablespoons of pasta water to blend. Reheat the pancetta over medium-high heat. Drain the pasta and add to the sauté pan with a few cranks of pepper and toss together.

○ To serve, divide between warm bowls and spoon the egg yolk mixture over the pasta. Sprinkle with grated pecorino and serve immediately.

Contains Starch: Pasta, Noodles, Grains, and Rice

Crab PAD THAI

This is really a crossover recipe that combines two of my favorite Thai dishes—tom yum and pad thai—and takes advantage of the Bay Area's famous Dungeness crab. Tom yum is a spicy, fragrant, hot-and-sour soup usually steeped with chiles, lemongrass, kefir lime leaves, ginger, and galangal, plus mushrooms and other vegetables. It's often served with chicken, tofu, or prawns and sometimes coconut milk. Pad thai, which is a growing popular Thai dish in this country, is usually made with rice noodles, dried shrimp, peanuts, lime juice, fish sauce, and bean sprouts. I like to merge these two dishes and give it a local (for me) twist by adding Dungeness crab—but other types of crabmeat work well, too. If I am on the East Coast, I will make it with fried soft-shell crab served on top. Kefir lime leaves, fish sauce, and bean sprouts can all be found in Asian markets.

SERVES 2

---

6 ounces dried Thai rice noodles or rice vermicelli

3 cloves garlic

1/4 cup canola oil

1 cup coconut milk

2 teaspoons sugar

1/2 teaspoon Sriracha hot sauce or red pepper flakes

2 tablespoons chopped peeled fresh ginger

2 kefir lime leaves

1/4 cup chopped fresh cilantro stems, plus leaves for garnish

2 green onions, sliced (white and green parts separated)

Salt and freshly ground black pepper

2 teaspoons Asian fish sauce

1 tablespoon soy sauce

1 Fresno chile, sliced into rings

1 lime, halved (reserve 1 half and cut the other into wedges)

1/2 cup mung bean sprouts

8 ounces Dungeness or other crabmeat, cooked

2 tablespoons roasted salted peanuts or cashews

8 Thai basil leaves

○ Soak the rice noodles in hot water for 10 to 15 minutes.

○ Slice 2 of the garlic cloves. In a sauté pan, heat the canola oil over high heat and fry the garlic until just light golden, 10 to 15 seconds. Strain the garlic and dry on a paper towel. Remove the garlic-infused oil from the heat and reserve.

○ In a saucepan, combine the remaining clove of garlic, coconut milk, sugar, hot sauce, ginger, kefir lime leaves, cilantro stems, the white part of the green onions, and a pinch of salt and bring to a boil. Remove from the heat, cover, and set aside for 15 to 20 minutes. Puree with an immersion blender in the pot or in a blender. Strain, and season to taste.

○ In the same sauté pan used for frying the garlic, heat the reserved garlic oil over high heat. Drain the noodles and add to the pan along with ¼ cup of the coconut milk–ginger puree, fish sauce, soy sauce, chile slices, juice of half the lime, and half of the bean sprouts. Sauté briefly, 1 to 2 minutes; add a few cranks of black pepper.

○ Spoon about ¼ cup of the coconut-ginger puree into the bottom of 2 bowls. Divide the noodles between the bowls, top with the crabmeat or half a crab per plate, and garnish with the fried garlic, peanuts, the remaining bean sprouts, cilantro leaves, basil, green part of the green onions, and lime wedges.

LINGUINE with WALNUT-BASIL PESTO, BROCCOLINI, and LEMON

When I have lots of basil, I make pesto (page 27). This is a no-brainer. I love pesto quickly tossed with hand-cut linguini and broccolini, with a little lemon and extra walnuts for texture. I also love the pesto tossed on gnocchi and just a little Parmesan grated over (page 122).

SERVES 4 AS AN APPETIZER OR 2 AS A MAIN COURSE

1 tablespoon salt

8 ounces Homemade Pasta (page 113) or 4 ounces dried linguine pasta

1½ cups chopped broccolini or broccoli (about 5 ounces)

¾ cup (6 ounces) Walnut-Basil Pesto (page 27)

Small wedge pecorino romano or Parmigiano-Reggiano cheese

1 tablespoon grated lemon zest (from a Meyer or regular lemon)

Freshly ground black pepper

2 tablespoons crushed walnuts

○ For the linguini, bring a large pot filled with water to a boil over high heat and add the 1 tablespoon salt. Drop in the pasta and cook for 4 minutes if using fresh pasta, or 8 minutes if using dried pasta. For the last 30 seconds of cooking, let the broccolini cook with the pasta.

○ In a large sauté pan over high heat, add the pesto and ¼ cup of the pasta cooking water. Drain the pasta and broccolini and add to the pan; toss for 1 minute.

○ To serve, divide the pasta-broccolini mixture among bowls, grate some of the cheese over, and sprinkle with the lemon zest. Season with a few cranks of black pepper and top with the walnuts.

Contains Starch: Pasta, Noodles, Grains, and Rice

My Mom's NOODLES with CHICKEN, CARROTS, and PEAS

My mom, Sherry, makes these thick noodles in chicken stock or broth for the holidays. She calls them holiday noodles. My brothers and I always ask just to double-check that she is making them when we get together for either Thanksgiving or Christmas. The heavy dusting of flour on them adds a thickness to the broth, so it really is a hearty side. I have added carrots, pearl onions, chicken, and peas so that it becomes more like a chicken pot pie but with noodles instead of pastry. It falls somewhere between a soup, a pasta, and a chicken and dumplings dish (or all of the above).

SERVES 4

1³/₄ cups all-purpose flour

3 teaspoons salt, plus more for seasoning

1 teaspoon baking powder

2 large eggs

¹/₂ cup heavy cream

1 tablespoon olive oil

4 baby carrots, or 1 large carrot cut into ¹/₂-inch pieces

¹/₂ cup pearl onions (about 6), halved lengthwise and peeled

1 boneless, skinless chicken breast (about 8 ounces), cut into ¹/₄-inch strips

3 cups Chicken Stock (page 30)

1 cup water

Freshly ground black pepper

Pinch of ground allspice

1 cup fresh or frozen (thawed) peas

2 tablespoons unsalted butter

1 tablespoon soy sauce

2 tablespoons Italian parsley leaves, whole or minced

○ To make the noodles, combine 1¹/₂ cups of the flour, 1 teaspoon of the salt, and the baking powder in a bowl. In another bowl, whisk the eggs and cream together until smooth and then add to the flour mixture. Stir with a spatula or spoon to moisten the flour.

○ Spread 2 tablespoons of the remaining flour on a work surface and dump the dough onto it; sprinkle the remaining 2 tablespoons flour over the dough. Knead the dough just so it comes together without feeling tacky or sticky. Roll out with a rolling pin ¹/₈ inch thick. Cut into 4 by ¹/₂-inch strips with a knife. Allow the noodles to rest and dry out for 1 hour.

○ In a large saucepan over medium heat, add the olive oil, carrots, and pearl onions and sauté for 2 minutes. Add the chicken, stock, and the 1 cup water and season with the remaining 2 teaspoons salt, a few cranks of pepper, and the allspice. Bring to a boil. Add the noodles. Cover, decrease the heat to a simmer, and cook for 3 minutes. Add the peas, butter, and soy sauce to the pot and cook for another 2 to 3 minutes. Season to taste.

○ Serve immediately with the parsley sprinkled over the top.

SHRIMP, ANDOUILLE, and GRITS

Sweet prawns, spicy smoked andouille sausage, and cheesy grits combine into serious comfort food to me. I am enamored with the South in general, and its food in particular, but especially with Louisiana—New Orleans is one of my all-time favorite cities. I buy Anson Mills or Bob's Red Mill grits. If you can get prawns with heads, use them!

SERVES 2

1 piquillo pepper, poblano chile, or red bell pepper

$^1/_2$ cup grits or polenta (either white or yellow, but not instant)

2 cups water

1 teaspoon salt, plus more as needed

1 tablespoon butter

$^1/_4$ cup grated Cheddar cheese

1 teaspoon Tabasco sauce

$^1/_4$ cup heavy cream

Freshly cracked black pepper

2 teaspoons olive oil

$^1/_2$ yellow onion, cut into $^1/_4$-inch slices

1 andouille sausage (about 3 ounces), cut into chunks or slices

2 cloves garlic, sliced

2 stems okra, sliced into disks

1 tomato, cut into dice (with skin and seeds)

$^1/_4$ teaspoon cayenne pepper

$^1/_2$ cup Chicken Stock (page 30)

8 large prawns

2 teaspoons freshly squeezed lemon juice

2 tablespoons fresh Italian parsley, whole leaves or minced

○ Char the pepper or chile over a flame until blackened all over. Put in a bowl and cover with plastic wrap or place in a bag in the refrigerator to sweat. Once cool, slip off the charred skin, core, and seed. Cut into $^1/_4$-inch slivers.

○ In a small saucepot, combine the grits, the 2 cups water, and the 1 teaspoon salt and bring to a boil over high heat. Decrease the heat to low and cook, stirring occasionally, for 30 minutes or according to the package instructions. Add the butter, cheese, Tabasco, and cream. Stir to melt the cheese. Season with salt and pepper. Cover and set aside; keep warm.

○ In a large sauté pan over high heat, add the olive oil. Add the onion and sweat for 1 to 2 minutes. Add the sausage, garlic, and okra and cook for 1 more minute. Add the roasted pepper or chile, tomato, cayenne, stock, and prawns. Cover and simmer for 3 to 4 minutes. Season to taste. Add the lemon juice and parsley.

○ Divide the warm grits between 2 bowls. Divide the sausage stew over the grits. Serve immediately.

RAMEN in MISO DASHI

There are just so many options for a making a big bowl of noodles. My favorite Japanese foods are kept simple and are not in your face with a lot of strong flavors. My version of miso broth and flavorings is kept to that simplicity here. You can substitute chicken stock for water, use chicken instead of pork, and add shreds of nori seaweed or fried garlic bits or even Kimchee (page 20) if you want to spice things up. You can find kombu, bonito flakes, miso paste, and togarashi at Asian markets. I enjoy having this dish for brunch.

SERVES 2

MISO DASHI (BROTH)

1 piece dried kombu (naturally preserved kelp), about 6 inches square

1-inch piece fresh ginger, sliced into coins

5 cups water

1 cup bonito flakes (dried, shaved bonito—a type of tuna)

1 tablespoon red miso paste

Salt and freshly ground black pepper

8 ounces dried or fresh udon noodles

1 tablespoon soy sauce

TOPPINGS

2 ounces enoki or shiitake mushrooms, sliced

4 ounces cooked pork tenderloin, thinly sliced

2 Soft-Boiled Eggs (page 12), halved lengthwise (optional)

2 green onions, sliced

2 tablespoons grated daikon radish

1 teaspoon toasted sesame oil

2 teaspoons togarashi (a chile-based Japanese spice blend)

○ To make the dashi, in a large saucepot, combine the kombu and ginger with the 5 cups water and bring to a boil over high heat. Turn off the heat and stir in the bonito and miso paste. Set aside.

○ Bring a pot of water to a boil and add a pinch of salt. Add the udon noodles and cook for 7 to 8 minutes for dried or 2 to 3 minutes for fresh. Drain.

○ Strain the dashi and return to the pot; bring to a simmer over low heat. Add the soy sauce and season to taste.

○ To serve, divide the noodles between 2 warm bowls. Arrange the mushrooms, pork, eggs, green onions, and grated daikon on top of the noodles. Pour the dashi into the bowls and finish with the sesame oil and togarashi.

○ Serve immediately.

CURRY and BLACK RICE

Like most everyone, when I get home I want to chill out and escape from my daily grind, and I do that with my food. When I cook, I feel like I can go on an adventure or travel somewhere else, at least for a moment. I've never been to India, but I have enjoyed exploring Indian spices and love that there is so much variety of flavor in its vegetarian cuisine. The curry spice blends vary among the different regions, so this is an American adaption with the spices that make up different blends in India. This is a very easy dish to make and I jazz up the plate with black rice, but basmati or other rice works great as well.

SERVES 4

CURRY SPICE BLEND

2 tablespoons ground turmeric

1 stick cinnamon or ^{1}/$_2$ teaspoon ground cinnamon

1 teaspoon cardamom seed

^{1}/$_4$ teaspoon whole cloves

^{1}/$_2$ teaspoon ground cumin

^{1}/$_2$ teaspoon fennel seed

^{1}/$_4$ teaspoon coriander seed

^{1}/$_4$ teaspoon fenugreek

^{1}/$_2$ teaspoon cayenne pepper

^{1}/$_4$ teaspoon freshly ground black pepper

RICE

1 cup black rice or basmati rice

2 cups water

1 teaspoon salt, plus more for seasoning

2 tablespoons brown butter (see page 17), divided

1 teaspoon saffron threads

^{1}/$_4$ cup chopped pistachios

1 small onion, cut into small dice

2 cloves garlic, minced

2 teaspoons minced fresh ginger

2 teaspoons Curry Spice Blend

1^1/$_2$ cups Chicken Stock (page 30) or purchased vegetable stock

1 teaspoon sugar

1 teaspoon molasses

2 teaspoons freshly squeezed lime juice, plus lime wedges for serving

1 large russet potato, peeled and cut into 1-inch chunks

3 carrots, cut into ^{1}/$_2$-inch pieces

1 rutabaga or turnip (about 10 ounces), peeled and cut into ^{1}/$_2$-inch pieces

^{1}/$_2$ head cauliflower or broccoli, cut into florets

^{1}/$_2$ cup coconut milk

^{1}/$_4$ cup plain whole-milk yogurt

4 sprigs fresh cilantro

○ For the spice blend, grind all the ingredients in a spice grinder and store, covered, in a cool, dark place. The curry will keep for up to a year, but it loses flavor over time. You can use a Madras curry blend, but it won't be as dramatic.

○ For the rice, in a small saucepan, add the rice, the 2 cups water, and a pinch of salt. Cover and bring to a simmer. Decrease the heat to low, and cook, covered, for 15 minutes. When done, stir in 1 tablespoon of the brown butter, the saffron, and the pistachios. Set aside.

(continued)

○ In a large saucepan over medium-high heat, add the remaining 1 tablespoon brown butter and the onion. Sauté or "sweat" for 2 to 3 minutes, then add the garlic, ginger, the 1 teaspoon salt, and the 2 teaspoons curry blend. Stir for 1 minute to release the oils in the spices. Add the stock, sugar, molasses, and lime juice and simmer for 15 minutes.

○ Meanwhile, place the potato, carrots, and rutabaga in a pot of cold water with a pinch of salt and bring to a boil over high heat. Decrease the heat to a simmer, cook for 5 minutes, and add the cauliflower. Cook until the vegetables are easily pierced with a knife, another 5 minutes. Drain and set aside.

○ Add the coconut milk to the curry and then all of the vegetables. Simmer for another few minutes.

○ To serve, place 1 tablespoon of yogurt in the bottom of each of 4 serving bowls. Spoon some of the rice into the bowl and then arrange vegetables around and on the rice and add some of the curry sauce around the bowl. Garnish with the cilantro leaves and stems and lime wedges. Serve immediately.

QUINOA with PARSNIP PUREE and PICKLED QUINCE

Eating a more vegetarian diet has become important to me. I absolutely believe that we need to eat and enjoy poultry, fish, and meat, but feel that we are totally overdoing it. I experiment with the not-so-familiar grains like teff, millet, and quinoa that are becoming more readily available. Quinoa is very high in protein and it's available in pale white, red, and black—all would work well in this dish. Despite the lack of meat, this dish is full of flavors and textures. It occurred to me to pickle quince after years of poaching it in sugar syrup for desserts or cooking it down into a paste. It's a great way to add depth to any dish. And the combination of pecans and Gouda rounds out the flavors.

SERVES 2 TO 4

PICKLED QUINCE

1 quince, peeled and cut into ¼-inch cubes

½ cup sugar

½ cup water

1 teaspoon salt

2 tablespoons red wine vinegar

3 whole black peppercorns

QUINOA

1 cup red, white, or mixed quinoa

2 cups water

Salt and freshly ground black pepper

3 parsnips (about 10 ounces total), peeled and cut into $1/2$-inch pieces

2 tablespoons unsalted butter

$1/4$ cup heavy cream

$1/4$ teaspoon pure vanilla extract

2 tablespoons olive oil

1 shallot, thinly sliced

1 cup mustard greens or kale, cut into ribbons

$1/4$ cup toasted pecans, roughly chopped

2 teaspoons freshly squeezed lemon juice

2 ounces smoked Gouda, cut into $1/4$-inch cubes

○ For the pickled quince, combine the quince, sugar, water, salt, vinegar, and peppercorns in a small saucepan and bring to a boil. Simmer until the quince is tender with a little crunch, about 20 minutes. Pour into a shallow dish to cool. It will keep in the refrigerator for up to 6 months.

○ For the quinoa, in a saucepan, combine the quinoa with the 2 cups water and a pinch of salt. Bring to a boil over high heat, decrease the heat to a simmer, and cook, covered, for 20 minutes.

○ While the quinoa is cooking, in a separate saucepan, add the parsnips and enough water to cover. Bring to a boil over high heat, then decrease the heat to a simmer and cook until soft, 15 to 20 minutes; drain. Puree in a blender with the butter, cream, vanilla, and a pinch of salt. Press through a strainer into a bowl. Season to taste with salt and pepper.

○ In a large sauté pan over high heat, add the olive oil and shallot and sweat for 1 minute. Add the cooked quinoa, mustard greens, pecans, salt and pepper, and lemon juice and toss for 15 seconds. Remove from the heat.

○ To serve, divide the parsnip puree between plates. Top with the quinoa mixture, the smoked Gouda, and the pickled quince.

135

THE MAIN COURSE

HERE ARE my all-time favorite main courses.

I have worked on trying to extract a lot of flavors in each of these recipes and have combined ingredients and components to make these standout dishes for any day of the week.

Grilled PORK CHOP with Sautéed APPLES and ONION RINGS

There are rubs (dry) and there are brines (wet). I love brining pork and chicken to make them juicy and flavorful. But brining is a slow process because the meat must sit in the brine for hours to overnight. If I am cooking late and didn't think about it the day before, I will do a nice rub on the meat to give it special flavor—and that's what I've done here. Pork chops go with so many accompaniments, but I do love them paired with the acidity of apples or an applesauce and the bite of spicy greens. I like onion rings, in all their variety. Here is a buttermilk recipe, but you can substitute the beer batter from Curried Fish and Chips (page 154).

My other favorite accompaniment to pork chops is the spicy Korean pickled vegetable Kimchee (page 20) tossed with some fresh fruit such as peaches or plums.

SERVES 2

PORK CHOPS

1/2 teaspoon fennel seed

4 whole cloves

1/2 teaspoon pimentón (Spanish smoked paprika)

1/2 teaspoon whole black peppercorns

2 teaspoons salt

1 teaspoon light brown sugar

2 bone-in, center-cut pork chops (10 to 12 ounces each)

1 tablespoon olive oil, if needed for the pan

SAUTEÉED APPLES

2 tablespoons sugar

1 tablespoon water

1 teaspoon freshly squeezed lemon juice

1 Granny Smith apple, cored and cut into 1/4-inch-thick slices

1 whole star anise

1 tablespoon unsalted butter

2 tablespoons brandy

Salt

ONION RINGS

3 cups canola oil, for frying

1/2 cup all-purpose flour

1/2 cup cornstarch

1/2 teaspoon salt, plus more as needed

Freshly ground black pepper

1/2 cup buttermilk

1 large yellow onion, cut into 1/2-inch rings and separated

Spicy greens like mizuna or arugula, for serving

○ For the pork, grind the fennel, cloves, pimentón, peppercorns, salt, and sugar in a spice grinder and rub all over the pork chops. Set aside for 30 minutes to 1 hour at room temperature.

(continued)

○ Preheat the grill on high or heat a cast-iron skillet over medium-high heat on the stove and preheat the oven to 375°F. (Add the 1 tablespoon olive oil to the pan if cooking on the stove.)

○ Cook the pork on one side for 4 to 5 minutes on the grill or on the stove. Turn over and cook for another 4 to 5 minutes on the grill; if cooking on the stove, flip the chop in the pan, transfer the pan to the oven, and bake for 4 to 5 minutes. Set aside to rest for 5 minutes.

○ For the apples, in a medium sauté pan over medium-high heat, combine the sugar, water, and a drop of the lemon juice. Cook until the sugar caramelizes to golden brown; turn off the heat and add the apple slices and star anise. Return the pan to medium-high heat and stir in the butter and the remaining lemon juice. Saute, stirring, for 2 minutes; add the brandy in the last minute of cooking with a pinch of salt. Simmer briefly to burn off the alcohol and thicken the caramel. Set aside.

○ For the onion rings, in a wide and shallow pot bring 2 cups of the canola oil to 360°F on a deep-fat thermometer.

○ Combine the flour, cornstarch, the 1/2 teaspoon salt, and a few grinds of pepper in a bowl. Pour the buttermilk into a shallow dish or bowl. Dip the onion rings in the flour mixture to dredge, shaking off any excess. Dip in the buttermilk to coat, and then back in the flour mixture. Shake off the excess flour.

○ Working in batches, fry the rings until light golden brown, about 3 minutes. Drain on paper towels and sprinkle with salt.

○ To serve, divide the apples between 2 plates and place a pork chop on top. Top with the onion rings and garnish with the greens.

PORK TENDERLOIN SCHNITZEL with PLUM GASTRIQUE

Schnitzel—breaded veal or pork cutlets—are classic dishes found everywhere on menus in Germany and Austria. I never liked the super-thin veal schnitzel and prefer pork. I've done it with pork loin, not flattened as much as the classic veal but just enough to give it a little more juiciness and higher proportion of meat to breading. Pork tenderloin is an easy cut of meat to work with. It is so tender and tasty and can be flattened easily and quickly. I made a version of pork schnitzel on *The Next Iron Chef* in 2011 and was quite happy with the results, as were the judges. The creamed corn and fennel is a good alternative to the potato salad that is the traditional side dish for schnitzel. The plums add the needed acidity. Or substitute peaches, cherries, grapes, or any fruit with a good acidity and less-forward berry notes.

SERVES 4

PORK SCHNITZEL

1 pork tenderloin (1 to 1¹/₂ pounds), cut into 4 equal pieces

¹/₄ teaspoon fennel seed, ground with a mortar and pestle

Salt and freshly ground black pepper

1 large egg, lightly beaten

1 cup panko (Japanese dried bread crumbs) or other dried bread crumbs

CREAMED CORN

2 tablespoons unsalted butter

1 tablespoon olive oil

Kernels from 2 ears white corn (about ¹/₂ cups)

1 bulb fennel, half coarsely chopped, the other half reserved

4 green onions, chopped

1 cup Chicken Stock (page 30)

Salt and freshly ground black pepper

2 sprigs thyme

2 sprigs tarragon

1 cup heavy cream

PLUM GASTRIQUE

3 red plums, halved and pitted

¹/₄ cup sugar

Seeds from 1 vanilla bean

¹/₄ cup red wine vinegar

¹/₄ cup canola or olive oil

○ For the pork, with a mallet or rolling pin, flatten the tenderloin pieces to about ¹/₂ inch thick. Rub the chops with the ground fennel, salt, and pepper to season.

○ Put the egg and bread crumbs in separate shallow dishes. Dip each tenderloin piece in egg and then press into the bread crumbs on both sides to adhere. Keep refrigerated until ready to cook.

○ For the creamed corn, heat the butter and oil in a sauté pan over medium heat. Add the corn, chopped fennel, and green onions, and sweat for 2 to 3 minutes. Add the stock and season with salt and pepper. Simmer until the stock is mostly evaporated, about 5 minutes; add the thyme, tarragon, and cream, decrease the heat to low, and simmer gently until the mixture is very thick and creamy, about 15 minutes.

○ For the gastrique, in a blender, puree 2 of the plums; set aside. In a small saucepan over medium-high heat, cook the sugar and vanilla bean until it melts and turns golden brown, swirling the pan occasionally.

○ Carefully pour in the vinegar and simmer 2 for minutes to dissolve the caramelized sugar. Add the plum puree, decrease the heat to medium-low, and simmer, stirring often, until thick and syrupy, about 10 minutes. Pour the mixture into a fine-mesh strainer set over a bowl or measuring cup and press the solids to extract as much liquid as possible. Discard the solids and set the gastrique aside until ready to serve.

○ To cook the pork, heat the canola oil in a sauté pan over medium-high heat. Cook the breaded schnitzel on each side until the breading starts to get crisp and brown, about 3 minutes. Keep warm in a low oven.

○ To serve, slice the remaining plum very thinly; using a mandoline (or very thinly slice with a knife), shave thin slices of the remaining 1/2 bulb fennel.

○ Divide the corn mixture among 4 plates and top with the schnitzel. Drizzle the gastrique around the corn and garnish with the shaved raw fennel and plum slices.

○ Serve immediately.

BEEF STROGANOFF with PARSLEY EGG NOODLES

When I think of beef stroganoff, the first image that comes to mind is a thickened disaster of pasta tossed with canned cream of mushroom soup topped with overcooked and chewy beef—which is absolutely why I wanted to address this dish. (Disclaimer: That is not what my mom ever made!) Short ribs or braised beef cheeks are your best meat choices here. This dish does take longer to prepare than most of the recipes in this book. But braised meat is better the next day or so after you make it because it really does need resting time. So, consider prepping this dish on a night you are cooking something else to eat and have it the next day. Alternatively, you can use flank or skirt steak to make a quick version of this dish.

SERVES 4

SHORT RIBS

4 large short ribs (about 2 pounds) or beef cheeks, or 8 ounces flank or hanger steak

Salt and freshly ground black pepper

2 tablespoons olive oil

$1/2$ onion, chopped

1 rib celery, chopped

1 carrot, chopped

2 cloves garlic, coarsely chopped

1 bay leaf

2 sprigs thyme

2 cups red wine or beer

2 tablespoons balsamic vinegar

3 tablespoons tomato paste

4 cups Beef Stock (page 31) or store-bought beef broth

STROGANOFF

$1/4$ cup crème fraîche or sour cream

1 tablespoon whole-grain mustard

$1/2$ teaspoon freshly grated nutmeg

Salt and freshly cracked black pepper

4 ounces fresh egg noodles, or 8 ounces dried egg noodles

3 baby or Thumbelina carrots, halved lengthwise

3 Tokyo turnips, halved, or 1 large turnip, cut lengthwise into 6 wedges

2 tablespoons olive oil

6 ounces chanterelles, oyster, or cremini mushrooms, sliced

2 tablespoons unsalted butter

8 fresh Italian parsley leaves

○ For the short ribs, preheat the oven to 300°F. Season the meat with salt and pepper. Heat the oil in a very large, wide Dutch oven over high heat. Sear the meat on all sides until browned and remove from the pan. Decrease the heat to medium and add the onion, celery, and carrot. Sweat, stirring, for 1 minute. Add the garlic, bay leaf, thyme, red wine, vinegar, tomato paste, and stock and bring to a simmer. Nestle the seared ribs into the liquid and add a hefty pinch of salt and pepper. Cover and cook in the oven for 4 hours. Lift out the ribs gently and strain the braising liquid and return half of it back with the ribs.

Let the short ribs cool completely in the braising liquid before refrigerating along with the strained liquid overnight.

○ If using hanger or flank steak, marinate the meat using the same amount of olive oil, garlic, bay leaf, thyme, and balsamic vinegar as for the short ribs, plus salt and pepper. Marinate for 30 minutes at room temperature and then grill on each side for about 4 minutes per side. Let the meat rest for 5 minutes and slice against the grain; set aside.

○ When ready to make the stroganoff, preheat the oven to 325°F. Remove the strained braising liquid and short ribs from the refrigerator and skim off the solidified fat on both and discard that fat. Wrap the ribs tightly in a double layer of aluminum foil along with its braising liquid. Place on a baking sheet and warm in the oven while you make the dish.

○ To make the sauce, put the strained reserved braising liquid in a small saucepan and bring to a simmer over medium heat. Cook until the liquid is reduced by three-fourths (to about 1 cup). Remove from the heat; whisk in the crème fraîche, mustard, and grated nutmeg. Season to taste with salt and pepper. Set aside.

○ Bring a large pot of water to a rolling boil and add enough salt for it to taste like the saltwater of the sea. If using fresh noodles, drop them into the water along with the carrots and turnips and cook for 4 minutes. If using dried, drop in the noodles, cook for 4 minutes, then add the carrots and turnips and cook until the noodles are al dente and the vegetables can be pierced easily with a knife, about 4 minutes more. Reserve 1/4 cup of the cooking water before draining the pasta in a colander.

○ Meanwhile, in a wide sauté pan, heat the olive oil over high heat and add the mushrooms. Decrease the heat to medium and cook until the water is released from the mushrooms and dries up, and the mushrooms are cooked, about 4 minutes. If the mushrooms are really wet, drain off the excess liquid released during cooking. Add the noodles, carrots, turnips, and the 1/4 cup reserved pasta cooking water to the sauté pan along with the butter. Sauté, stirring, until the water is absorbed, another 1 to 2 minutes.

○ To serve, divide the noodles and vegetables among 4 large bowls or plates. Set 1 short rib next to the noodles. Spoon some of the sauce over the ribs and noodles. Garnish with the parsley and serve immediately.

RIB EYE on the Grill

When I shop for beef for myself I often buy for more than one meal. Usually, I will cut up an 8-ounce steak into two or three portions and then freeze what I don't use for the next time. I don't eat big portions of beef, generally speaking. A few bites work for me. A rib eye is a great cut because the fat around the meat gives it flavor and juiciness. I simply season with salt and pepper. If I'm feeling totally decadent, then I make potatoes with sour cream and brown butter (see page 17) and some wild arugula to go with, or douse it with Steak Sauce (page 24) or Horseradish Cream (page 20), with some rapini (page 162) on the side. I like a medium-rare steak: if you like yours rare, cook for a minute less on each side; for medium, cook an additional minute per side.

SERVES 2

8-ounce rib-eye steak, about 1 inch thick
   (see Note, following)

$^1/_2$ teaspoon salt

Freshly ground black pepper

Small pinch of red pepper flakes

○ Let the meat sit out at room temperature for at least 20 minutes.

○ Preheat the grill to high heat.

○ Season the meat all over with salt, black pepper, and red pepper flakes. Grill on one side until nicely caramelized with dark grill marks, about 4 to 5 minutes. Turn over and grill for another 4 to 5 minutes.

○ Let the steak rest for 5 minutes, then slice the meat and divide between 2 plates.

○ Serve with just about any of the side and supporting dishes in chapter 8 (page 159).

Note: I prefer to cook the whole 8-ounce steak, let it rest, and then slice it for 2 servings. But you can also cut the steak in half down the middle before you cook it and serve two 4-ounce portions.

NEW YORK in Cast Iron

A New York steak (aka strip steak, shell steak, and others, depending on where you live) is a lean cut, so I really want to serve it with béarnaise sauce because it's rich from all that butter that's emulsified with the vinegar and egg yolk. Equally indulgent would be a side of Duck Fat Fries (page 175) or chips (page 154). For something green, try the haricots verts (page 161). Hey, if you want more meat, use a bigger piece.

SERVES 2

8-ounce New York strip steak, about 1 inch thick (see Note, following)

2 tablespoons olive oil

Sprig of rosemary

1 clove garlic, sliced

$1/2$ teaspoon salt

Freshly ground black pepper

○ Drizzle the steak with the olive oil and scatter the rosemary and garlic slices on the steak. Season with salt and pepper and rub all over. Set aside for 20 minutes.

○ Heat a cast-iron skillet over high heat. Add the steak and decrease the heat to medium. Cook for about 3 to 4 minutes per side for medium. Let the steak rest for 5 minutes, then slice the meat and divide between 2 plates.

Note: I prefer to cook the whole 8-ounce steak, let it rest, and then slice it for 2 servings. But you can also cut the steak in half down the middle before you cook it and serve two 4-ounce portions.

A BURGER

A burger. It's obviously one of the best sandwiches ever invented. Period. I actually never make the same recipe twice. Sure, I have tendencies, but honestly, I like to explore. This is the kind of burger recipe to build on, trying different combinations or condiments and cheese or bun options. Of course, you can use any cheese you like, but I love the notes of nut and caramelized milk in Comté or Raclette. The buns are important! I don't like an overly buttery bun because I find it just too rich with everything else on the burger. I like a pretzel roll, milk bun (aka white bun), or ciabatta. I prefer my burger medium-rare but cook a few minutes less for rare and a few minutes more for medium.

SERVES 2

8 ounces lean (but not the leanest) ground beef

2 strips smoked bacon, finely chopped (optional)

2 teaspoons minced fresh lovage or Italian parsley

1/2 teaspoon salt

Freshly ground black pepper

2 slices (about 1 ounce each) Comté, Raclette, or Gruyère cheese

2 pretzel, brioche, or milk bread buns, halved

2 tablespoons Mayonnaise (page 22) or store-bought

2 teaspoons Dijon mustard

2 teaspoons grated fresh horseradish

2 tablespoons pickled shallots

○ Preheat the grill to high heat or heat a cast-iron skillet over high heat on the stove.

○ In a bowl, combine the ground beef, bacon, and lovage. Roll the meat into 2 balls and flatten into 1-inch-thick patties. Set aside for 5 minutes (or more). Before grilling, season both sides with salt and lots of freshly ground pepper.

○ For either the grill or the cast-iron pan, decrease the heat to medium and add the hamburger patties. Cook for 3 to 4 minutes on one side. Flip over and cook for another 3 minutes for medium-rare. Top with the cheese, cover the grill or pan, and cook for another minute, until the cheese melts.

○ Remove from the heat while toasting the buns. Place the buns, cut sides down, on the grill or in the cast-iron pan (or in a toaster oven) and toast until light golden. Spread the bottom halves of the buns with the mayonnaise and the tops with the mustard and horseradish. Put a burger on each bun bottom, top with some pickled shallots, and close the bun. Enjoy.

CHILAQUILES with FRIED EGG

These tortilla chips coated in smoky chiles, onion, and tomato salsa, with beans and cheese on the side are addictive! This becomes a great vegetarian dish just by swapping vegetable stock for the chicken stock. I top it with a fried egg to make it a filling dish for any time of day or night. One of my favorite versions is at Mijita, the San Francisco taqueria of Traci Des Jardins. This isn't Traci's recipe, but it's definitely inspired by my many Saturday or Sunday morning cravings at Mijita after going to the Ferry Plaza farmers' market, where one branch of the restaurant is located.

SERVES 2

2 poblano chiles

2 tablespoons olive or canola oil, plus more for frying the eggs

1/2 onion, cut into small dice

1 cup Roasted Tomato–Chipotle Salsa (page 23) or other salsa

1/2 cup Chicken Stock (page 30)

1/2 ripe avocado, peeled, pitted, and cut into 1/2-inch pieces

3 cups corn tortilla chips (about 3 ounces)

1 cup canned refried beans

Dash of hot sauce of your choice

Salt and freshly ground black pepper

2 large eggs

3 tablespoons crumbled cotija cheese or ricotta salata

2 tablespoons crème fraîche or sour cream

1/2 lime, cut into wedges

2 sprigs cilantro

○ Roast the chiles over a hot grill or over the flame on a gas stove or in a 400°F oven until blistered. Put the peppers in a bag, or in a bowl and cover with plastic wrap, and refrigerate for 15 minutes to sweat. Remove the blackened skin. Core and remove the seeds. Cut into ribbons.

○ In a large sauté pan, heat the 2 tablespoons olive oil over medium heat. Add the onion and sweat for 2 minutes. Add the chile strips and the salsa and bring to a simmer. Add the stock and simmer for 2 minutes. Add the avocado and tortilla chips and coat evenly and quickly. Warm the beans in a separate saucepan with the hot sauce; season with salt and pepper.

○ In a nonstick pan, heat 1 to 2 teaspoons oil over medium heat. Crack the eggs in the pan and fry, sunny side up. Season with salt and pepper.

○ To serve, spoon some of the beans onto each plate. Add the chilaquiles and then the fried eggs. Top the beans with the cheese and a dollop of crème fraîche. Garnish with the lime and cilantro.

Brined ROASTED CHICKEN in Parts

A brined chicken is far tastier than one that isn't brined. I add the breasts about half-way through so they don't overcook. When I do roast this much chicken, I can use the cooked chicken for several other dishes during the week. I put the parts in the brine before I go to work. When I get home, I then drain off the brine and let the chicken come to room temperature for at least 20 minutes before roasting.

SERVES 2 TO 4

1 small whole free-range roaster chicken
   (about 3 pounds)

BRINE

2 tablespoons sugar

3 tablespoons salt

4 cups water

Freshly ground black pepper

2 tablespoons olive oil

4 cloves garlic

2 sprigs thyme

2 bay leaves

1 lemon, quartered

Salt and freshly ground black pepper

○ To butcher the chicken, I like to use a cleaver, but a sharp chef's or boning knife will also work. Begin by making a cut down the center of the breast along one side of the sternum bone and cut down the rib cage to free the breast meat. Do the same on the other side of the sternum bone to free the other half of the breast. Now make a cut where the wing is attached and snap down to free the wing. Cut through the ligaments that attach it. Repeat with the other wing. Make a cut at the leg where the thigh bone and snap the leg where it is attached at the ball joint. Cut around the top of the joint and free the leg. Do the same on the other side. Similarly, make an incision where the thigh is attached to the drumstick. You will have to cut through the ball joint. Cut through each thigh as close as you can to the backbone.

○ For the brine, dissolve the sugar and salt in the 4 cups water and add a few grinds of black pepper. Add the chicken parts, cover, and refrigerate for 12 to 24 hours.

○ Preheat the oven to 500°F. Drain the chicken parts, pat them dry thoroughly with paper towels, and let them stand at room temperature for at least 20 minutes.

○ Heat the oil in a large cast-iron or heavy skillet over high heat. When the oil is very hot and rippling, add the chicken legs, thighs, and wings, skin side down. Add the garlic, thyme, bay leaves, and lemon wedges. Season with salt and pepper. Decrease the oven to 450°F place the pan in the oven, and roast for 20 minutes. Turn the pieces over and move toward the sides of the pan to make room for the breasts. Add the chicken breasts, skin-side down, and return to the oven for another 15 minutes. Turn the breasts over and roast for a final 5 minutes. Pull the pan out of the oven.

○ Let the chicken rest, slightly covered, for 5 minutes before serving.

CURRIED FISH and CHIPS

Frying fish in a batter coating is a great way to seal in the juices. It also creates a dramatic contrast in texture between the crunchy exterior and the hot, flaky fish inside. I was in London for a semester in college and at that time, the best food was served at the fish and chips shops and the Indian restaurants. Those flavors and experiences must be embedded in my memory—those new-wave, punk-filled club nights mixed with curries and early morning fish and chip munchies. The curry salt dusted on the chips mixed with the saffron and ginger of the mayo is a crossover of those flavors all playing off of each other.

SERVES 2 TO 4

DIPPING SAUCE

1/4 cup Mayonnaise (page 22) or store-bought

1/4 teaspoon saffron

1/2 teaspoon finely grated peeled fresh ginger
  (use a Microplane grater)

CHIPS

1 large russet potato (about 12 ounces)

1 tablespoon olive oil

4 cups canola oil, for frying

Salt

1/4 to 1/2 teaspoon Curry Spice Blend
  (page 133), for dusting

FISH

1/4 cup all-purpose flour

2 tablespoons cornstarch

Pinch of salt

1/4 cup beer or club soda

10 ounces cod, halibut, bass, or other type of
  white fish, cut into 4 equal portions

○ Preheat the oven to 400°F.

○ For the sauce, whisk the mayonnaise, saffron, and ginger together. Set aside.

○ For the chips, halve the potato lengthwise and cut each half lengthwise into 6 steak fry wedges. Rinse the potatoes under cold water until the water runs clear. Pat dry with paper towels.

○ On a baking sheet, toss the potatoes with the olive oil and bake in the oven for about 20 minutes.

○ Heat the canola oil in a heavy pot to 360°F on a deep-fat thermometer over high heat. Working in batches, drop in the potatoes and fry until golden brown, 3 to 4 minutes. Remove with a slotted spoon and drain on paper towels. Season with salt. Keep the oil at 360°F.

○ For the fish batter, whisk the flour, cornstarch, salt, and beer together in a bowl.

○ Dip the fish into the batter, letting any excess drip off. Fry in the hot oil until golden brown, 4 to 5 minutes. Drain briefly on paper towels.

○ To serve, divide the fish between plates. Add the fries and dust with the Curry Spice Blend. Serve with the saffron-mayonnaise dipping sauce.

FALAFEL

The best falafel I've ever had is at Tiam in New York City's West Village. It was beyond memorable because it was so fluffy and light. Eating there inspired me to come up with my own version of falafel. You must have the Tahini Sauce (page 25) with this and I also enjoy it with Harissa (page 19), Greek yogurt, chopped cucumbers, and fresh parsley leaves. I don't care for store-bought pita, so some grilled flatbread made with the Pizza Dough (page 98) or warmed naan or lavash bread is also good.

SERVES 4

1 teaspoon cumin seed

$^1/_2$ teaspoon coriander seed

$^1/_4$ teaspoon fenugreek seed

$^1/_4$ teaspoon red pepper flakes

2 cups chickpeas, cooked

$^1/_2$ white onion, coarsely chopped

2 cloves garlic

2 tablespoons white sesame seed

$^1/_4$ cup matzo meal

2 tablespoons chopped fresh Italian parsley

1 teaspoon baking powder

1 large egg

2 teaspoons salt

Freshly ground black pepper

4 cups canola oil, for frying

FOR SERVING

Tahini Sauce (page 25)

Grilled flatbread

Harissa (page 19)

Cucumbers, chopped

Olives

Parsley

Cilantro

Lemon

○ Grind the cumin, coriander, and fenugreek seed and red pepper flakes together with a mortar and pestle or in a spice grinder. Set aside.

○ In a food processor, combine the chickpeas, onion, garlic, and the ground spices, and pulse several times to mince everything. Add the sesame seed, matzo meal, parsley, and baking powder and pulse until evenly mixed but not a puree. Whisk the egg in a large bowl. Add the chickpea mixture, salt, and a few cranks of black pepper. Refrigerate for a minimum of 15 minutes.

○ Line a baking sheet with parchment paper. Roll the chickpea mixture into 16 golf ball–size balls and flatten each slightly. Heat the canola oil in a heavy pot to 360°F on a deep-fat thermometer over high heat. Fry the falafel, in batches if necessary, turning in the hot oil as they fry, until golden, 2 to 3 minutes. Drain on paper towels.

○ Serve hot with the Tahini Sauce, grilled flatbread, yogurt, Harissa, and any combination of cucumbers, olives, parsley, and cilantro. Add a squeeze of fresh lemon juice.

SIDEKICKS AND SUPPORTING DISHES

THERE ARE TIMES when I get home and will start to prepare something more substantial like a steak or roasted chicken with a side dish, and then I just get hungry for the side dish and eat it before my main course is ready. Some of these sides are the **sidekicks and supports to a main course,** or could be elaborated into a satisfying appetizer or served next to a pasta or a main course. The rapini and kale dishes are great as a side to Spaghetti and Meatballs (page 119) or Brined Roasted Chicken in Parts (page 153). The Corn Succotash is perfect with the Grilled Pork Chop (page 139). Mashed Potatoes and Potatoes Mousseline are great with just about anything. Cherry Tomato Confit can dress up any plate but can also be tossed with pasta or into a salad. Duck Fat Fries are good alone but even better with a New York in Cast Iron steak (page 148) or a Burger (page 151).

HARICOTS VERTS with WALNUTS, SHALLOTS, and CREAM

This side goes with just about everything. I cook the beans on the al dente (crisp-tender) side because the crunchy bite of green beans goes well with the cooked shallots and the richness of walnuts and cream. Haricots verts are small French green beans and have a-stronger flavor compared to that of wax beans or other string beans; however, those will work here, too.

SERVES 4

1 teaspoon salt, plus more for seasoning

1 pound haricots verts (French green beans), trimmed

1 tablespoon olive oil

2 shallots, minced

1/2 cup walnuts, crushed

2 teaspoons freshly squeezed lemon juice

3 tablespoons heavy cream

1/2 teaspoon finely grated lemon zest (use a Microplane grater)

Freshly ground black pepper

○ Bring a large pot of water to a boil over high heat and add the 1 teaspoon salt. Drop in the beans and cook for 3 minutes; drain and set aside.

○ In a large sauté pan, heat the olive oil over medium heat. Add the shallots and walnuts and cook, stirring, for 3 minutes. Add the beans to the sauté pan along with the lemon juice and stir for 30 seconds. Add the cream and lemon zest and let the liquid bubble until the cream is slightly thickened and hot, about 30 seconds. Season with salt and pepper and serve immediately.

RAPINI with CHILE and MEYER LEMON

I like to present rapini (another name for broccoli rabe) as a really straightforward dish. Blanch rapini or broccoli, or any green in the broccoli family, in salted boiling water for less than a minute depending on thickness. Toss in olive oil, a little Fresno chile or red pepper flakes, and the grated zest and juice of a lemon or Meyer lemon if you can get it. Add garlic or anchovy for a little more action. Or add toasted pine nuts and currants for more textural contrast.

SERVES 4

Salt

2 tablespoons extra-virgin olive oil

Finely grated zest of 1/2 a lemon or Meyer lemon

Juice of 1 lemon or Meyer lemon

1/2 teaspoon red pepper flakes or 1 Fresno chile, stemmed and sliced

1 bunch rapini or broccoli rabe or any member of this family, stem ends chopped off and the rest chopped into 1-inch pieces

1/2 teaspoon Maldon flake salt or kosher salt

Freshly ground black pepper

○ Bring a large pot of water to a boil. Add enough salt so that it tastes like the saltwater of the sea.

○ In a bowl, whisk the olive oil, lemon zest and juice, and red pepper flakes or Fresno chile together until combined. Drop the rapini into the boiling water and blanch for 30 seconds. Drain, shaking the colander forcefully to remove as much water as possible, and transfer to the bowl with the dressing.

○ Toss well, transfer to a serving dish, and sprinkle with the Maldon salt and a few cranks of black pepper. Serve immediately.

KALE, Two Ways

One of my favorite ways to eat kale is cut into thin strips (chiffonade) and blanched in boiling water, shocked in ice water, drained, dried, and tossed with a vinaigrette as I have here in the First Way.

Kale is often sautéed, as I have done here in the Second Way, and I have added bacon, molasses, and a little garlic.

EACH SERVES 4

First Way

1 bunch kale (about 12 ounces)

Salt and freshly ground black pepper

2 tablespoons sherry vinegar

2 tablespoons maple syrup

2 teaspoons freshly squeezed lemon juice

1/2 teaspoon finely grated lemon zest

1 shallot, minced

3 tablespoons olive oil

○ Trim off the long ends of the stems of the kale but leave the inner stem intact. Stack the kale leaves into one pile and cut them crosswise into 1/4-inch-wide ribbons (chiffonade).

○ Have an ice bath (a bowl of ice water) ready. Bring a large pot of water to a boil and add a heavy pinch of salt. Drop the kale into the boiling water and blanch for 15 to 20 seconds. Drain and immediately put in the ice water to stop the cooking. Drain and spin in a salad spinner or dry completely with a clean kitchen towel.

○ Whisk the vinegar, syrup, lemon juice and zest, and shallot together in a bowl. Add a pinch of salt and pepper and whisk in the olive oil. Toss the vinaigrette with the kale and serve as a side. It's also great with the addition of pine nuts or pistachios or grapes (or all of them).

Second Way

1 large bunch kale (about 1 pound)

1 tablespoon olive oil

2 slices bacon, cut into 1/4-inch pieces

2 shallots, sliced

1 clove garlic, thinly sliced

1 tablespoon freshly squeezed lemon juice

2 teaspoons molasses

Salt and freshly ground black pepper

1 tablespoon unsalted butter, if needed

○ Trim off the woody stems of the kale but leave the inner stem intact. Stack the kale leaves into a pile and cut them crosswise into 1-inch-wide ribbons (chiffonade).

○ In a large sauté pan, add the olive oil and bacon over high heat. Cook until the edges of the bacon are just beginning to brown and the fat is rendered, 2 to 3 minutes. Decrease the heat to medium, add the kale leaves, sprinkle with the shallots, and cover. Cook until just cooked through, about 3 to 4 minutes. Remove the lid, toss the kale well with tongs, and add the garlic, lemon juice, and molasses. Cover again and cook for another 5 minutes. Uncover, toss, and cook until the juice is mostly abosorbed, another 1 to 2 minutes. Season with salt and pepper. Add a tablespoon of butter if the mixture is dry. Serve immediately.

Asian COLESLAW

Coleslaw is great alongside so many main courses, but the word *coleslaw* doesn't sound sexy. The word *slaw* sounds sloppy to me. That aside, try it with the curried Fish and Chips (page 154) or the Hot Wings with Habanero BBQ Syrup (page 75) or as a side with any fish dish. Hijiki seaweed can be found in Asian markets, health food stores, and often in supermarkets these days.

SERVES 2 TO 4

1/2 cup hijiki (Japanese seaweed)

2 teaspoons minced peeled fresh ginger

1 tablespoon rice wine vinegar

1 tablespoon freshly squeezed lime juice

1/2 teaspoon ground turmeric

1 teaspoon sugar

1 teaspoon toasted sesame oil

2 tablespoons canola or olive oil or Mayonnaise (page 22)

2 cups shredded cabbage

1 cup shredded carrot

3 green onions, cut on the extreme diagonal

1 tablespoon sesame seed

○ To rehydrate the hijiki, cover with hot water and set aside for 15 minutes, covered. Drain.

○ Whisk together the minced ginger, rice wine vinegar, lime juice, turmeric, sugar, and sesame oil. Whisk in the oil or mayonnaise. Toss with the cabbage, seaweed, and carrot. Top with the green onions and sesame seed. The slaw will keep for 3 days covered in an airtight container in the refrigerator.

Sidekicks and Supporting Dishes

CORN Succotash

Succotash usually consists of lima beans, corn, and other vegetables, and is traditionally served in a casserole on the side. We get more fava beans than lima beans in Northern California, so that's what I use, or sometimes black-eyed peas. I serve this with pork, halibut, or chicken. I like the cream in succotash, but chicken stock is another alternative depending on what you serve it with.

SERVES 4

2 tablespoons olive oil

$1/2$ onion, chopped

1 clove garlic, minced

Fresh sweet corn kernels, cut from 3 cobs (about 2 cups)

1 cup fresh fava beans, peeled, or black-eyed peas

$1/4$ cup heavy cream or Chicken Stock (page 30)

1 tablespoon minced fresh Italian parsley

2 teaspoons fresh thyme leaves

$1/4$ teaspoon cayenne pepper

2 tablespoons unsalted butter

Dash of Tabasco sauce

1 teaspoon salt

Freshly ground black pepper

○ In a large sauté pan over high heat, add the olive oil. Add the onion and sweat, stirring, until soft but not brown, 3 to 4 minutes. Add the garlic and the corn kernels and sauté for 3 minutes. Add the fava beans, cream, parsley, thyme, and cayenne. Add the butter, Tabasco, the 1 teaspoon salt, and a few cranks of black pepper. Simmer over medium heat, stirring, until thickened, 2 to 3 minutes. Taste and adjust the seasoning with salt and pepper.

○ Serve hot.

CHERRY TOMATO Confit

These are great to use instead of tomato sauce for a quick pasta, as a side to a steak, added to a salad, or as a side with eggs for breakfast. Served on crostini with a little ricotta, they make a great snack or hors d'oeuvre.

MAKES ABOUT 1 CUP

2 cups cherry tomatoes

3 cloves garlic

2 sprigs thyme

1 sprig rosemary or marjoram

$^1/_2$ cup olive oil

1 teaspoon salt

$^1/_2$ teaspoon sugar

Freshly ground black pepper

○ Preheat the oven to 300°F. In a Dutch oven or baking dish, combine the whole cherry tomatoes, garlic, herb sprigs, and olive oil. Sprinkle with the salt, sugar, and a few cranks of black pepper. Cook in the oven for about 50 minutes. Remove from the oven and set aside to come to room temperature. Cool completely before storing in the refrigerator for up to 1 week.

Roasted CORIANDER CARROTS

The combination of coriander, cilantro, honey, and orange zest makes these roasted carrots a great accoutrement to just about anything. This dish gives a nod to Moroccan and Mediterranean flavors.

SERVES 2 TO 4

8 medium carrots, with tops

1 tablespoon olive oil

$1/2$ teaspoon crushed coriander seed

$1/4$ teaspoon grated orange zest

Salt and freshly ground black pepper

2 tablespoons unsalted butter, at room temperature

2 teaspoons honey

1 tablespoon fresh cilantro leaves, minced

○ Preheat the oven to 400°F.

○ Wash the carrots but do not peel them. Trim off the tops, but leave $1/4$ inch of the stem intact. Scrub right around the stems and top stub of the carrots. Leave the root intact.

○ Put the carrots, olive oil, crushed coriander seed, and orange zest in a large baking dish; season with salt and pepper. Toss the carrots to coat with the oil. Cover with aluminum foil and roast until a knife inserted into the thickest part of a carrot meets little resistance, 20 to 30 minutes, depending on their thickness. Remove the foil cover and continue to roast for another 5 minutes.

○ Meanwhile, in a small bowl, mix together the butter, honey, cilantro, and a pinch of salt.

○ When the carrots are done, set on a serving plate or divide between plates, and top with some of the cilantro butter.

Mashed POTATOES

Buttermilk adds creaminess and also a bit of tang to these mashed potatoes. Add a little blue cheese to these for a knock-out side. Add an extra pat of butter, if you want, to the top of the finished potatoes, and let it melt over for even more lusciousness.

SERVES 4

2 russet potatoes (about 1³/₄ pounds), peeled and cut into 1-inch chunks

4 to 5 cups water

4 tablespoons (¹/₂ stick) unsalted butter

³/₄ cup buttermilk

Salt and freshly ground black pepper

○ Rinse the potatoes under cold water. Combine the potatoes with 4 to 5 cups water in a saucepan and bring to a boil over high heat. Decrease the heat to a vigorous simmer. Cook the potatoes until a knife pierced in the potatoes meets no resistance, about 10 minutes. Drain well and pass the potatoes through a ricer. Or use the paddle attachment in a stand mixer or a handheld mixer, or mash with a fork or potato masher. Set the riced potatoes and butter in a saucepan over low heat; stir to dissolve the butter. Add the buttermilk and season with salt and pepper. Serve immediately.

POTATOES MOUSSELINE

When I worked at Masa's in San Francisco in the early 1990s, I discovered potatoes mousseline, which is about equal parts butter to potato—why they are so damn good! You can also add shaved black or white truffle, which may bring you to tears.

SERVES 4 TO 6

2 large russet potatoes (about 2 pounds), peeled and cut into 1-inch chunks

1¹/₄ cups (2¹/₂ sticks) unsalted butter

¹/₄ cup heavy cream

Salt and freshly ground black pepper

○ Cook the potatoes as above, and then pass through a ricer. In a saucepan over low heat, add 4 tablespoons of the butter to the potato puree and stir to thoroughly combine. Add the cream and another 4 tablespoons butter, stirring well to combine. Continue adding butter, 4 tablespoons at a time, stirring well and melting the butter completely before adding more, until all the butter is used. Season with salt and pepper. Serve immediately.

DUCK FAT FRIES

Duck fat gives potatoes a savory richness and the fat has a high smoking point, so it is great for frying and gives the fries a crispy exterior. I like to blend the duck fat with peanut or canola oil so the fries are not overwhelmed with duck fat flavor. We have served Duck Fat fries at Orson since we opened. I love it with our lemony Brown Butter Béarnaise (page 17), which is better than ketchup for the extra savoriness that the duck fat gives to the fries. French fries need to be blanched to cook the interior of the fries and start the sealing in of the moisture inside. Fried a second time, they become crisp and delicious.

SERVES 2 TO 4

2 large russet potatoes (about 2 pounds)

1¹/₂ cups canola or peanut oil

1 cup rendered duck fat

Salt

4 fresh sage leaves

Brown Butter Béarnaise (page 17), for serving

○ Wash and dry the potatoes. Halve the potatoes lengthwise. Put a potato half on a cutting board, cut side down, and cut lengthwise into ¹/₄-inch slices. Working a couple of slices at a time, turn the slices onto their flat side, and cut lengthwise again into ¹/₄-inch batons. Repeat with the remaining potatoes. Rinse under cold water and set on paper towels to dry for at least 10 minutes.

○ For the first fry, combine the oil with the duck fat in a heavy pot. Heat the fats to 325°F on a deep-fat thermometer. Drop the potatoes into the oil in batches and cook without browning until the potatoes are just barely tender, about 3 minutes. With a wire-mesh or slotted spoon, remove the parcooked fries from the hot oil and set on clean kitchen or paper towels to drain and cool. You can freeze the potatoes at this point, which makes them even better on the final fry.

○ For the second fry, bring up the oil to 360°F. Drop the potatoes into the oil in batches and fry until golden brown and crisp, 3 to 4 minutes. Remove from the oil and drain again on clean kitchen or paper towels and sprinkle with salt. Fry the sage leaves at the end for a few seconds and drain. Crumble onto the fries.

○ Serve immediately with the béarnaise sauce for dipping.

Baked MARBLE or YUKON GOLD POTATOES with Brown BUTTER– SOUR CREAM SAUCE

Marble potatoes are very small potatoes—the size of, well, marbles! They are some-times sold in a mix of colors—white, rose, and purple. I make this fun side dish into a starter when I serve it with shaved radishes and caviar. The side and the starter variation are both an homage to my friend, the chef and amazing writer Gabrielle Hamilton, who makes a dish I have had a few times with brown butter, radishes, and trout roe. Typical Gabrielle—a magic touch with just a few ingredients. If you want to turn it into a starter, use four or five radishes, thinly shaved or quartered, and a spoonful of caviar or trout roe per person.

SERVES 2 TO 4 AS A SIDE DISH OR STARTER

2 cups marble or Yukon gold potatoes

2 tablespoons olive oil

1 teaspoon salt, plus more for seasoning

Freshly ground black pepper

$^1/_2$ cup sour cream

2 tablespoons browned butter (see page 17), warm but not hot

○ Preheat the oven to 400°F.

○ Add the potatoes and olive oil to a cast-iron skillet or a baking sheet and toss to coat. Sprinkle with the 1 teaspoon salt and some pepper. Roast until the potatoes are soft inside, but not mushy or browned, 10 to 15 minutes.

○ In a small bowl, add 1 tablespoon of the sour cream and whisk in the brown butter. Whisk in the rest of the sour cream and season with salt.

○ Serve a shmear of the sauce on plates with the potatoes scattered over.

CHICKPEAS with MIDDLE EASTERN SPICES

I found some black chickpeas grown in Montana recently, which make a crazy cool colored hummus, but any dried chickpeas will work here. If you don't want to take the time to soak and cook dried chickpeas, you can use canned, which are already cooked.

SERVES 4

1 cup dried chickpeas

4 cups water

Salt and freshly ground black pepper

1 tablespoon olive oil

1/2 cup chopped onion

1 clove garlic, sliced

1/4 teaspoon toasted and ground cumin seed

Pinch of saffron

2 teaspoons Harissa (page 19) or store-bought

1/4 cup chopped tomato

1 roasted red pepper, skinned, seeded, and sliced into strips (see poblano chiles page 152)

Squeeze of fresh lemon juice

○ To cook the chickpeas, combine the dried chickpeas and 3 cups of the water in a large container or bowl and soak overnight. As the chickpeas absorb water, they will expand.

○ Drain off the water and put the chickpeas in a saucepan. Add enough water to cover the chickpeas by 2 inches and a pinch of salt and cook over a gentle simmer for about 30 minutes. Turn off the heat, cover, and let sit for 5 minutes. Drain and store the chickpeas in cold water, covered, in the refrigerator until ready to use.

○ In a large sauté pan over medium heat, add the olive oil. Add the onion and sweat, stirring, for 3 minutes. Add the garlic, cumin, and saffron; stir. Add the harissa, tomato, and pepper; stir for another minute. Add the 1 cup cooked chickpeas and the remaining 1 cup water and season with salt and pepper. Simmer until the water nearly evaporates and the liquid thickens, about 4 minutes. Add the lemon juice and taste to finish seasoning. Serve.

Roasted BEETS

I never seem to get tired of eating beets. I love their flavor and their colors (especially the red ones), and I particularly love to eat them with horseradish and crème fraîche. I make a raita (the traditional Indian cucumber-yogurt sauce) with roasted and grated beets mixed with yogurt and cumin to use as a condiment. I also like them with goat cheese and marinated in a little red wine or balsamic vinaigrette. I use baby red beets with grilled beef heart in a salad and with braised beef short ribs. I slice large red beets, dip them in a tempura batter, and fry them up to serve with steak tartare and horseradish ice cream. I thinly slice roast beef for a sandwich with large slices of pickled red beets and Horseradish Cream (page 20). Sometimes I make beet juice mixed with apple, rosemary, and lemon in the morning. If I were a vegetarian vampire, this would be my blood of choice.

SERVES 2 TO 4

4 red beets

2 teaspoons olive oil

1/2 teaspoon salt

Freshly ground black pepper

2 teaspoons water

Freshly squeezed lemon juice or aged
  balsamic, for serving

Extra-virgin olive oil, for serving

○ Preheat the oven at 425°F. Trim the leaves off the beets, but leave about a 1/2 inch of stem and the root intact. Wash the beets and then set them in a small Dutch oven or ovenproof casserole. Add the olive oil, salt, a little pepper, and the water to the pot. Cover and bake until a knife slips in a beet easily, about 30 minutes.

○ Cool slightly and remove the skins, which should slip off easily. Squeeze a little lemon juice over or a drizzle of an aged balsamic and a drizzle of extra-virgin olive oil and season to taste with more salt and pepper, and let the beets speak for themselves.

DESSERTS FOR DREAMING

THESE ARE my home-style desserts

that I hope will blow your friends and family away—from drinkable desserts to cookies, a couple of takes on pie, a devilish chocolate cake, and some special ice creams. Sometimes when I have a party at home, or am cooking for friends, or with my family, I serve dessert much later in the evening, after we have had too much to drink and lots of food. I like to **finish off the evening with something that sums up the day.** These desserts came from my heart so that my guests can feel my love for them and everyone can sleep well.

Malted Rich HOT CHOCOLATE

This is a dessert in its own right. A combination of milk and dark chocolate mixed with Ovaltine and malt powder is like a malt ball candy, without being overly sweet. If you use carob, it also has a rich malty flavor. Before I was seven years old, I couldn't eat chocolate because I was allergic to it, so I was given carob instead, now it is a nostalgic flavor that I crave every so often. For a bit more indulgence, I finish it with a spoonful of whipped cream, even though it is rich enough without it.

SERVES 2

2 tablespoons carob or cocoa powder,
   or 1 tablespoon each

1 tablespoon sugar

1 tablespoon Ovaltine

2 teaspoons malt powder

Pinch of salt

2 cups whole milk

1 ounce bittersweet chocolate, finely chopped

1 ounce milk chocolate, finely chopped

$1/4$ cup heavy cream, whipped to soft peaks
   with a drop of pure vanilla extract

○ In a medium saucepan, combine the carob, sugar, Ovaltine, malt powder, salt, milk, and chocolates over low heat and bring to a gradual simmer while whisking. Pour into 2 mugs and top each with a dollop of whipped cream. Enjoy immediately.

Dark Mint HOT CHOCOLATE

Now this is what I want après-ski or when I am just dreaming of skiing but am stuck at home. At ski lodges, I have always been served peppermint schnapps mixed with weak hot cocoa, but this recipe is jacked up with bittersweet chocolate, mint extract, and bourbon—which gives this hot chocolate a lot more depth.

SERVES 2

2 tablespoons cocoa powder

2 tablespoons sugar

$1/4$ teaspoon pure vanilla extract

$1/2$ teaspoon pure mint extract

2 cups whole milk

$1/4$ cup heavy cream

2 ounces bittersweet chocolate, finely chopped

2 tablespoons bourbon

○ In a medium saucepan, combine the cocoa, sugar, vanilla, mint, milk, cream, and chocolate over low heat and bring to a gradual simmer while whisking. Stir in the bourbon. Enjoy immediately.

Bourbon Pecan Pie MILKSHAKE

When I thought about "cookies and cream" as a flavor, I had an aha! moment. "Cake shakes!" "Pie shakes!" I wanted to make milkshakes with the flavors of some of my cake and pie recipes. No pecan pies are sacrificed to make this milkshake. It's all about delivering pecan pie flavors in a tall, cool glass of thick and creamy goodness.

SERVES 2

1 cup vanilla ice cream

$1/2$ cup whole milk

2 teaspoons cane syrup or molasses

1 teaspoon honey

Pinch of salt

2 tablespoons toasted pecan halves

$1/2$ cup crumbled shortbread cookies

2 tablespoons bourbon

○ Combine all the ingredients in a blender and process until smooth. Serve immediately.

CACAO NIB CHOCOLATE
Sandwich Cookies

Several years ago, I wanted to come up with a few sandwich cookies for Citizen Cake that would be tasty versions of popular, commercially made cookies—Oreos were one. But I wanted mine to use fresher and better ingredients. We sell this in three versions: chocolate (this recipe), ginger, and lemon. This is the ultimate cookie with an ice-cold milk for a late-night dessert.

MAKES 16 SANDWICH COOKIES

COOKIES

$^3/_4$ cup unsalted butter ($1^1/_2$ sticks), at room temperature

$^1/_2$ cup granulated sugar

1 teaspoon pure vanilla extract

1 cup all-purpose flour, plus more for dusting

$^1/_2$ cup plus 2 tablespoons unsweetened cocoa powder

$^1/_4$ cup cacao nibs, very finely chopped

$^1/_2$ teaspoon kosher salt

FILLING

4 tablespoons unsalted butter, at room temperature

1 cup confectioners' sugar, sifted

$^1/_4$ teaspoon pure vanilla extract

Pinch of kosher salt

○ For the cookies, in the bowl of a stand mixer fitted with the paddle attachment, cream the butter, granulated sugar, and vanilla at high speed until light and fluffy, 2 to 3 minutes. Decrease the speed to low, add the flour and cocoa powder, and mix until the dough comes together. Add the cacao nibs and salt and mix 1 more minute. Flatten the dough into a disk, wrap tightly in plastic wrap, and refrigerate for 30 minutes.

○ Meanwhile, make the filling. In the bowl of a stand mixer fitted with the paddle attachment, combine the butter and confectioners' sugar and mix until smooth. Add the vanilla and salt and mix for 1 more minute. Transfer to a bowl, cover tightly with plastic wrap, and set aside at room temperature.

○ To bake the cookies, preheat the oven to 325°F. Line 2 baking sheets with parchment paper. Dust a work surface with flour and with a rolling pin, roll out the chilled dough to $^1/_4$ inch thick. Cut out thirty-two 2-inch rounds with a cookie cutter and place them on the lined baking sheet. Bake until set, 15 to 18 minutes. Transfer to a rack to cool completely.

○ To fill the cookies, spread or pipe a heaping teaspoon of filling on 16 cookies. Top with the remaining 16 cookies.

○ Store the cookies in an airtight container in a cool place or in the refrigerator. They'll keep for a week if they last that long.

Desserts for Dreaming

EGGNOG-A-RITA

This is eggnog as a cocktail, not a punch. I created it about twenty years ago (yikes!) for a holiday party. I had always thought eggnog needed to be very cold to be very good, and as a Californian, I have certainly had many a margarita, but this drink has a skirt of sugar and nutmeg rather than the salt used in a margarita. Although I had margaritas in mind at the time, this drink has no tequila, because, honestly, tequila, eggs, and cream don't sound good together. The trick for me that makes this really special is the combination of brandy, bourbon, and rum. They all have unique flavors that are very delicious combined with the custard base and fresh nutmeg shaken up on ice and strained and served very cold. Careful—two of these are easy to drink and powerful. A note: The better the booze, the better the cocktail.

MAKES 2 COCKTAILS

1 cup whole milk

1 cup heavy cream

Freshly grated nutmeg

4 large egg yolks

$^{1}/_{2}$ cup plus 2 tablespoons sugar

$^{1}/_{2}$ teaspoon pure vanilla extract

Pinch of ground cinnamon

Beaten egg white or a wedge of lemon, for finishing

4 tablespoons bourbon

4 tablespoons rum

4 tablespoons brandy

○ Combine the milk, cream, and a few gratings of nutmeg in a saucepan and bring to a boil over medium-high heat. Whisk the yolks and $^{1}/_{2}$ cup of the sugar together in a bowl. While whisking, slowly add the hot milk mixture to the yolks. Pour the mixture back into the saucepan and cook over low heat, stirring constantly with a spatula or a wooden spoon, until it just starts to thicken, 3 to 4 minutes. The mixture should coat the back of the spoon and cling to it. Strain, and add the vanilla. Chill until very cold.

○ Combine the remaining 2 tablespoons sugar and a pinch of nutmeg and cinnamon in a dish. Moisten the rims of 2 coupe glasses (shallow, bowl-shaped Champagne glasses), rocks glasses, or wine glasses with egg white or lemon juice and then roll in the sugar and spice mixture. In a cocktail shaker, add $^{3}/_{4}$ cup of the custard base and then the bourbon, rum, and brandy. Add ice and shake well. Strain the cocktail into the 2 glasses. Enjoy immediately.

VANILLA ICE CREAM with TANGERINES and AVERNA DATES

This dessert is an homage to one of the most amazing and influential restaurateurs, food activists, and culinary pioneers of all time—Alice Waters. At her Chez Panisse Café, in Berkeley, in the winter months, my favorite dessert is the Kishu tangerines and Barhi dates, both California-grown. When Alice is there, which is often, and she has brought the fruit to our table herself, I feel like a starstruck teenager. I am in awe of Chez Panisse and I continue to go there often and take other chefs there often. Alice always serves only the best that is available of these two fruits. Honestly, tangerines in season and dates from Southern California are like candy and need only the simplest presentation to show them off. I also love Medjool or Deglet dates, which are easier to find. Sometimes dates from the store shelf can be a bit dry, so I have cooked them in a little Averna amaro, an Italian bitter liqueur made from herbs, aromatics, and citrus rinds. When warm, the dates are fantastic with tangerines and a little vanilla ice cream. I've got a recipe here for vanilla ice cream, but in a pinch, just buy something yummy. I also like to candy the tangerine peel, which is especially great to prepare this way because it has little of the bitter pith (the white layer beneath the colored peel).

MAKES ABOUT 3 CUPS ICE CREAM; SERVES 4

VANILLA ICE CREAM

1 cup whole milk

1 vanilla bean, split and seeds scraped
  (save the pod for another use)

$1/2$ cup turbinado sugar

1 cup heavy cream, chilled

$1/2$ teaspoon salt

TANGERINES AND DATES

2 tangerines

$4^{1}/4$ cups water

Pinch of salt

1 cup granulated sugar

1 cup Medjool, Bahri, or other dates, pitted
  (about 8)

$1/2$ cup Averna amaro

○ For the ice cream, combine the milk, vanilla seed, and turbinado sugar in a saucepan and bring to a boil. Turn off the heat and stir to dissolve the sugar. Add the cold cream and the salt. Refrigerate or chill in an ice bath (a large bowl of ice water) until cold. Freeze in an ice cream machine according to the machine's instructions. Keep covered in the freezer for up to a month.

○ For the candied tangerine peel, remove the tangerine rind in large segments. Cut the rind into very thin julienne strips. Bring 2 cups of the water to a boil in a saucepan and add a pinch of salt. Add the tangerine strips and blanch for 30 seconds; strain. Mix 1 cup of the remaining water with $1/2$ cup of the granulated sugar, and bring to a boil. Add the blanched tangerine strips and simmer on low for 30 minutes; strain.

○ Bring 1 cup of the remaining water mixed with the remaining $1/2$ cup sugar to a boil and add the strips. Continue to simmer until the tangerine strips are tender to bite through. Turn off the heat and let the strips cool in the syrup.

○ The candied tangerine strips will keep in the syrup stored in a covered container for up to 9 months in the refrigerator for best flavor. Alternatively, you can strain off the syrup and let the strips dry out overnight on a wire rack. They can be rolled in sugar mixed with a pinch of citric acid and stored in a covered container in the pantry for up to 3 months for best flavor. Use them whole, dip in chocolate, chop and mix into cookie dough, use to decorate a cake, or just eat.

○ To make the dates, cut the pitted dates into 3 or 4 pieces. Combine them with the Averna and the remaining $1/4$ cup water in a skillet over high heat. Bring to a boil; carefully tip the pan to ignite the alcohol from the flame of a gas burner, and let the alcohol burn briefly (flambé). You can ignite the liqueur with a long lighter or match if working on an electric stove top. Turn off the heat and cover to extinguish the flame. Keep covered for 5 to 10 minutes. These will keep, covered in an airtight container, in the refrigerator for up to 1 month.

○ To serve, place a spoonful of Averna dates and their liquid in bowls. Add a couple of scoops of ice cream to each bowl. Pull apart the tangerine segments and divide among the bowls. Garnish the ice cream with a couple of candied tangerine strips. Serve immediately.

BLACK OLIVE ICE CREAM with CHOCOLATE-ORANGE SAUCE

Despite the saltiness of the olives, this does not come off as a salty dessert. Dry-cured olives are also very fruity and I don't add any salt to the chocolate sauce. The fruity notes in the chocolate with a touch of orange zest make this a surprising and exciting dessert combination.

MAKES 3 CUPS ICE CREAM; SERVES 4

1 recipe Vanilla Ice Cream (page 188), or 1^1/$_2$ pints high-quality store-bought

2 tablespoons very finely minced dry-cured pitted black olives

4 ounces bittersweet chocolate

^{1}/$_2$ cup heavy cream

2 tablespoons water

2 tablespoons corn syrup

^{1}/$_4$ to ^{1}/$_2$ teaspoon grated orange zest mashed with a pinch of sugar

2 tablespoons olive oil, plus more if desired

○ For the ice cream, follow the recipe for the ice cream with or without the vanilla bean. Fold in the minced olives when removing the ice cream from the machine. Or, if using purchased ice cream or previously frozen ice cream, remove the ice cream from the freezer and let soften at room temperature until scoopable, but not melting. Mix in the minced olives and refreeze until ready to serve.

○ For the sauce, chop the chocolate and set in a bowl. Combine the cream, the 2 table-spoons water, corn syrup, and orange zest in a saucepan and bring to a boil over medium-high heat. Pour over the chopped chocolate and set aside for a few minutes. Whisk gently until smooth. Add the 2 tablespoons olive oil to the chocolate sauce. You can also add a few drops of water to make a thinner sauce if desired.

○ Scoop the ice cream into bowls. Drizzle with sauce and additional olive oil, if desired.

PEANUT BUTTER–COCONUT Cookies

If you have ever had a candy bar called "Chick-O-Stick," then you'll understand my inspiration here. In my early carob-eating days, it was the one chocolate-free candy I liked. I think my first was pulled off one of the shelves at my great-grandfather's filling station in Big Spring, Texas. It was like a Butterfinger, but with a thin coating of micro-shredded coconut instead of chocolate. I wanted to make a drop cookie with this same flavor combination of peanut butter and coconut. This is what I came up with—and it's my new favorite cookie!

MAKES ABOUT 4 DOZEN

$3/4$ cup ($1^1/2$ sticks) unsalted butter, at room temperature

1 vanilla bean, split

$1^1/2$ cups rolled oats

2 teaspoons baking soda

$1^1/2$ cups granulated sugar

1 cup packed light brown sugar

1 cup creamy peanut butter

2 large eggs, at room temperature

$2^1/2$ cups all-purpose flour

$1^1/2$ cups unsweetened coconut

2 teaspoons kosher salt

○ Preheat the oven to 350°F. Line 2 baking sheets with parchment paper.

○ Melt half of the butter in a sauté pan over medium heat. Scrape the vanilla bean seeds into the butter. Add the oats and cook, stirring frequently, until browned and fragrant, about 5 minutes. Add the baking soda, stir to combine, and set aside to cool completely.

○ In the bowl of a stand mixer fitted with the paddle attachment, cream the remaining butter with the sugars and peanut butter at medium speed until light and fluffy, about 3 to 4 minutes. Add the eggs, one at a time, mixing well after each addition, about 1 minute each time. Decrease the speed to low and add the flour, coconut, and salt and mix until combined. Fold in the cooled browned oats until evenly dispersed.

○ Roll the dough into golf ball–size rounds (about 1 tablespoon dough each). Place the rounds about 1 inch apart on the lined baking sheets and bake until just golden, 12 to 15 minutes. Cool for 5 minutes on the sheets, and then transfer to a rack to cool completely. Repeat with the remaining dough.

○ Store the completely cooled cookies in an airtight container at room temperature.

CHOCOLATE CAKE with SALTED PEANUTS

I came up with this chocolate cake because I wanted a new cake to put on the menu at Epic Roasthouse. Jan Birnbaum, a friend of mine, is the chef at this steakhouse along San Francisco's waterfront. I was consulting on the dessert menu and thought he really needed a big piece of chocolate cake to be the signature chocolate dish. I served it with bourbon ice cream, caramel sauce, and salted pecans, but here I use salted peanuts.

SERVES 6 TO 8

CAKE

1 heaping cup all-purpose flour

$1/2$ cup cocoa powder

2 teaspoons baking powder

$1/4$ teaspoon baking soda

$1/2$ teaspoon kosher salt

2 ounces bittersweet chocolate, chopped

$3/4$ cup granulated sugar

$1/4$ cup molasses

$1/2$ cup canola oil

2 large eggs

$1/2$ cup buttermilk

2 tablespoons strong brewed coffee or espresso

$1/2$ teaspoon pure vanilla extract

NUTS

1 cup unsalted Spanish peanuts

2 teaspoons peanut or canola oil

1 teaspoon Maldon salt or sea salt

FROSTING

6 ounces bittersweet chocolate, chopped

4 ounces milk chocolate, chopped

$3/4$ cup heavy cream

5 tablespoons corn syrup

$1/2$ teaspoon pure vanilla extract

$1/2$ teaspoon kosher salt

1 tablespoon bourbon

1 cup (2 sticks) unsalted butter, at room temperature

2 cups confectioners' sugar, sifted

$1/2$ cup unsweetened cocoa powder

○ For the cake, preheat the oven to 325°F. Grease a $12^1/2$ by $17^1/2$-inch baking sheet and line with parchment paper. Sift together the flour, cocoa powder, baking powder, baking soda, and salt into a bowl; set aside.

○ Put the chocolate in a bowl and set over a a saucepan of simmering water until melted. Remove from the heat. Add the granulated sugar, molasses, and canola oil to the chocolate and whisk together. Add the eggs and whisk until smooth. Add the buttermilk, coffee, and vanilla and whisk until smooth. Add the flour mixture and whisk into the wet ingredients to make a smooth batter.

○ Pour the cake batter into the lined baking sheet and bake until a toothpick inserted into the center comes out clean, about 20 minutes. Cool completely and invert onto a cutting board. Carefully peel off the parchment paper and invert back into the pan once it's completely cool.

○ Keep the oven at 325°F. For the nuts, toss the nuts with the 2 teaspoons oil and 1 teaspoon salt, spread out in a pan or on a baking sheet, and roast until fragrant and toasted, about 15 minutes. Cool completely and set aside.

○ For the frosting, combine the chocolates in a bowl and set the bowl over a simmering saucepan of water until it begins to melt, 1 minute. Stir until it is mostly melted, then remove from the heat.

○ In another saucepan, bring the cream and corn syrup to a simmer over medium heat, pour over the chocolate, and set aside for 5 minutes. Whisk gently until smooth and add the vanilla, salt, and bourbon. Set aside to cool completely, stirring occasionally.

○ In a stand mixer fitted with the paddle attachment, whip the butter, confectioners' sugar, and cocoa powder together on medium speed until light and fluffy, about 4 to 5 minutes. Decrease the speed to low, pour in a bit of the completely cooled chocolate mixture, and whip until combined. Continue adding chocolate to the frosting, scraping down the bowl occasionally, until the frosting is evenly mixed and fluffy. *Note:* Do not mix the hot ganache (chocolate-cream mixture) into the butter-sugar mixture. The ganache must be completely cool (but not cold) before mixing in.

○ To build the cake, immediately spread half of the frosting over the cooled cake. Chill the cake and the remaining unused frosting for 30 minutes. Remove the cake and frosting from the refrigerator and rewhip the frosting in the bowl if necessary.

○ Halve the cake crosswise in the pan. With 2 large spatulas, lift one of the cake halves and set it directly on top of the other. Cut the cake in half again and stack the layers. Frost the sides and top with the rest of the frosting. Cover with the roasted salted Spanish peanuts or just serve with the salted peanuts on the side. Keep covered in a cool place or in the refrigerator.

BLACKBERRY COBBLER with CREAM

I love making a cobbler on a warm summer night, especially around the Fourth of July. It is typically foggy in San Francisco in July, but ripe blackberries baked in a cobbler transport me to a veranda somewhere else where I can *see* the fireworks, not just hear them. With its simple top crust made of biscuit-dough squares that you just set on the filling, a cobbler is easier to make than a pie and is a nonfussy dessert. This is one of those soul-smackers and I see that when I make this, people react like I've kissed them on the forehead and tucked them into bed.

SERVES 4 TO 6

BISCUIT TOPPING

1 cup all-purpose flour, plus more for dusting

1/4 cup sugar

1 teaspoon baking powder

1/2 teaspoon kosher salt

1/4 teaspoon baking soda

4 tablespoons cold unsalted butter, diced

2 tablespoons buttermilk

2 tablespoons heavy cream

FRUIT FILLING

3 cups fresh blackberries

1/3 cup sugar, plus extra for sprinkling on the biscuits

1/2 teaspoon grated lemon zest

1 tablespoon tapioca flour, cornstarch, or all-purpose flour

Pinch of kosher salt

4 tablespoons unsalted butter, diced

1 large egg

1 tablespoon water

Heavy cream, for serving

○ Preheat the oven to 325°F.

○ For the biscuit topping, combine the flour, sugar, baking powder, salt, and baking soda in a bowl. Work the cold butter into the flour with your fingertips until it forms pea-size clumps. Add the buttermilk and cream and stir gently with a rubber spatula until a shaggy dough forms. Set aside while you make the filling.

○ For the filling, in a bowl, combine the blackberries, sugar, lemon zest, tapioca, and salt. Toss lightly. Pour into a 1-quart ceramic or other baking dish. Dot with the butter.

○ Dust a work surface with flour, and with a rolling pin, roll out the biscuit dough to 1/2 inch thick. With a sharp knife, cut into 2-inch blocks. Set on top of the berries. Whisk the egg and water together and brush the biscuits with the egg wash. Sprinkle with the sugar and bake until the filling is bubbling and the biscuit topping is golden, 35 to 40 minutes. Let stand for 15 minutes before serving.

○ Serve in bowls and pass a pitcher of heavy cream to pour on.

Sticky TOFFEE PUDDING with CREOLE CREAM CHEESE

This dessert is a merging of cultures. Sticky toffee pudding from England and Australia, made with dates and a toffee sauce, is divine on its own. But served with a Creole cream cheese from Louisiana, which is simple to make, it's even better. Creole cream cheese is a little like crème fraîche but with rennet added. Rennet is an enzyme used in cheese making that coagulates and separates the curd and whey. You can substitute crème fraîche if you don't feel like making the cream cheese.

SERVES 5 OR 6

CREOLE CREAM CHEESE

4 cups heavy cream

$1/2$ cup buttermilk

2 drops rennet (animal or vegetable derived)

PUDDING

$1^1/_4$ cups water

1 teaspoon baking soda

4 ounces dates, pitted and chopped (about 16)

4 tablespoons ($1/2$ stick) unsalted butter, at room temperature

$1/2$ cup packed light brown sugar

$1/2$ cup cane syrup

2 large eggs

$1^1/_2$ cups all-purpose flour

1 tablespoon baking powder

$1/4$ teaspoon kosher salt

STICKY TOFFEE SAUCE

4 tablespoons unsalted butter

1 cup heavy cream

$1/2$ cup plus 2 tablespoons packed dark brown sugar

$1/4$ cup cane syrup

$1/4$ teaspoon pure vanilla extract

$1/4$ teaspoon kosher salt

Cane syrup, fresh pecans, and Maldon salt, for serving

○ For the cream cheese, in a large stainless steel or glass bowl, combine the cream, buttermilk, and rennet. Cover the bowl with cheesecloth or a clean kitchen towel and set aside at room temperature for 24 hours. Cover with plastic wrap and chill. This mixture can be drained to thicken or stirred and used in its more liquid state. It will keep for 3 weeks in an airtight container in the refrigerator.

○ For the pudding, preheat the oven to 325°F. Butter an 8 by 4-inch loaf pan and set aside. Bring the $1^1/_4$ cups water to a boil and add the baking soda; pour over the dates in a bowl and set aside to cool.

○ In a stand mixer fitted with the paddle attachment, cream the butter, light brown sugar, and cane syrup on medium speed until fluffy. Add the eggs, one at a time, beating well and scraping down the bowl between additions. Sift the flour, baking powder, and salt together and add to the mixer; mix on low speed until combined. Pour in the date-water mixture (make sure it is completely cooled) and mix on low speed until smooth. Pour the batter into the prepared loaf pan and bake until set, about 40 minutes. Let cool completely in the pan before turning out onto a plate.

○ For the sauce, combine the butter, cream, dark brown sugar, and cane syrup in a medium saucepan and bring to a boil over medium-high heat. Decrease the heat to medium-low and simmer until slightly thicker, 8 to 10 minutes. Remove from the heat and stir in the vanilla and salt. Let cool until just warm for serving.

○ To serve, smear some of the Creole cream cheese on plates or in bowls. Slice or spoon some of the baked pudding onto each plate. Spoon over some toffee sauce and garnish with a little more cane syrup and some fresh pecans. (I also like to sprinkle a few grains of Maldon salt on top.)

CHERRY PIE, Two Ways

I am always renaming my desserts, so it seems strange for me to call something simply "Cherry Pie." I want to call it "Can She Bake a Cherry Pie" or "Che, Che, Cherry Bomb." But sometimes it is best to call it what it is. I have two versions here: the first is the classic double-crust cherry pie and the second is quicker to make and has all the same components but is made into four individual desserts.

Version I

MAKES ONE 9-INCH PIE

PIE DOUGH

$1^1/_2$ cups pastry flour, plus more for dusting

1 cup cake flour

$1/_2$ teaspoon kosher salt

$3/_4$ cup ($1^1/_2$ sticks) cold unsalted butter, diced (or half butter and half lard)

$1/_4$ cup ice water

2 tablespoons heavy cream

CHERRY FILLING

4 cups fresh cherries, pitted and halved (about $1^1/_2$ pounds)

1 cup plus 2 teaspoons sugar

3 tablespoons tapioca flour or cornstarch

$1/_4$ teaspoon pure almond extract

$1/_2$ teaspoon balsamic vinegar

1 large egg beaten with 1 teaspoon water, for glazing

Ice cream or whipped cream, for serving (optional)

○ For the dough, combine the flours and salt in a large bowl. Quickly work the cold butter into the flour with your fingertips until coarse crumbs form, leaving a few larger flakes. If using half lard and half butter, work in the lard first and then the butter, leaving a few larger pieces of butter. Combine the ice water and cream and work into the dough quickly, just to moisten. Flatten the dough into a disk and wrap in plastic wrap. Chill for at least 30 minutes. Cut the dough in half.

○ For the bottom crust, dust a work surface with flour, and with a rolling pin, roll out half of the dough into a 12-inch round that is $1/_4$ inch thick. Drape the dough around the rolling pin and lay over a 9-inch pie pan. Press the dough into the pan with your fingertips. Trim the edge to a 1-inch overhang all around. Put the trimmings with the other half of the dough. Refrigerate the bottom crust and the remaining half of the dough for 30 minutes.

○ For the filling, in a large bowl, combine the cherries, the 1 cup sugar, tapioca, almond extract, and balsamic vinegar and toss together. Pour the pie filling into the chilled pie shell.

(continued)

○ For the top crust, roll out the other half of the dough into a 12-inch round that is ¼ inch thick. Drape the dough around the rolling pin and lay over the pie. Trim the edge to match the overhang of the bottom crust. Fold the dough layers over (as one) to seal the pie. With your thumb and forefinger, pinch a decorative fluted pattern around the edge. Chill the pie for another 20 minutes.

○ Preheat the oven to 375°F. Snip three holes near the center of the top crust. Brush the pie crust (including the edges) all over with the egg wash. Sprinkle with the remaining 2 teaspoons sugar. Set the pie on a baking sheet and bake until golden brown, about 1 hour and 15 minutes. Cool for at least 30 minutes or more before cutting.

○ Serve with ice cream or whipped cream if desired.

Version II

MAKES 4 INDIVIDUAL DESSERTS

○ Make the dough as in Version I (page 201) and chill. Preheat the oven to 350°F and line a baking sheet with parchment paper. Cut the dough in half; freeze one half for another use. Dust the work surface with flour, and with a rolling pin, roll out the dough half into a 12-inch round that is about ¼ inch thick. With a 4-inch round cookie cutter, cut out 8 circles from the dough. Transfer the dough rounds to the lined baking sheet and prick the dough with a fork in a few spots on each round. Brush with the egg wash and sprinkle with the sugar. Bake until light golden brown, 20 to 25 minutes.

○ For the filling, combine the cherries and 1 cup sugar in a saucepan. Bring to a simmer over medium-low heat and cook until the cherries are softened, 6 to 8 minutes. In a small bowl, whisk the tapioca with 2 tablespoons water to make a slurry. Add the cherries and stir while simmering. Add the almond extract and balsamic vinegar. Cook, stirring, for another 1 to 2 minutes, until the mixture is very thick. Pour into a container to cool.

○ To serve, set a round of baked pastry on each of 4 plates or wide bowls. Spoon some of the cherry pie filling onto each pastry. Top each with another piece of pastry and serve with ice cream, whipped cream, or a drizzle of heavy cream.

APPLE PIE, Two Ways, (Apple of My Eye Pie)

I do love all kinds of apple pie. We only make apple pie in quantity in the bakery at Thanksgiving, and this first version is it. The pimentón give the cheese streusel a wonderful smokiness that pairs well with the apples. The second version is a quicker way to make a pie and produces four individual desserts. The filling uses apples that have been sautéed in Calvados, to boost its "apple-ness," and there's Cheddar cheese in the streusel.

Version I

MAKES ONE 9-INCH PIE

CHEDDAR STREUSEL

1 cup pastry flour

3 tablespoons cornstarch

1 tablespoon confectioners' sugar

$^1/_2$ teaspoon kosher salt

Pinch of pimentón (Spanish smoked paprika)

$^1/_2$ cup (1 stick) cold unsalted butter, diced

3 ounces grated Cheddar cheese (about $^3/_4$ cup)

$^1/_2$ recipe Pie Dough (page 201)

APPLE FILLING

$^1/_2$ cup granulated sugar

2 heaping tablespoons all-purpose flour

$^1/_2$ teaspoon fine salt

1 teaspoon ground cinnamon

$^1/_4$ teaspoon freshly grated nutmeg

4 Granny Smith apples, peeled, cored, and sliced

$^1/_4$ teaspoon pure vanilla extract

Ice cream or whipped cream, for serving (optional)

○ For the streusel, in a bowl, combine the flour, cornstarch, confectioners' sugar, salt, and pimentón and stir to combine. Quickly work the cold butter into the flour mixture with your fingertips until the butter is evenly distributed, with pieces still remaining. Add the cheese, stir to mix well, and squeeze the mixture to create clumps, from pea-size to quarter-size. Chill.

○ For the crust, preheat the oven to 350°F. Dust a work surface with flour, and with a rolling pin, roll out the pie dough into a 12-inch round that is $^1/_4$ inch thick. Drape the dough around the rolling pin and lay over a 9-inch pie pan. Trim the edge to a 1-inch overhang all around. Fold the dough over all around the pan and use your fingers to pinch a decorative fluted pattern around the edge.

○ For the filling, in a small bowl, combine the granulated sugar, flour, salt, cinnamon, and nutmeg. In a large bowl, combine the sliced apples and flour mixture, tossing to coat the (continued) apples evenly. Add the vanilla and toss. Pour the apples into the pie crust. Scatter the chilled streusel evenly over the pie and set it on a baking sheet.

○ Bake until the filling is bubbling and the streusel and crust are golden brown, 1 hour to 1 hour and 15 minutes. Cool for at least 30 minutes before slicing. Serve with ice cream or whipped cream, if desired.

Version II

MAKES 4 INDIVIDUAL DESSERTS

1 recipe Cheddar Streusel (page 203), chilled

1/2 recipe Pie Dough (page 201), chilled

1 large egg beaten with 1 teaspoon water, for glazing

1 to 2 teaspoons granulated sugar

APPLE FILLING

2 tablespoons unsalted butter

2 tablespoons light brown sugar

3 tablespoons granulated sugar

4 Granny Smith or other tart apples, peeled, cored, and sliced

1 cinnamon stick

1/4 teaspoon freshly grated nutmeg

Pinch of kosher salt

1/4 cup Calvados

1 tablespoon dry white wine or freshly squeezed lemon juice

Whipped cream or ice cream, for serving (optional)

○ Preheat the oven to 350°F. Line 2 baking sheets with parchment paper. Pour the chilled streusel onto one of the lined baking sheets and bake until golden brown, about 20 minutes. Set aside.

○ Dust the work surface with flour and roll out the dough into a 12-inch round about 1/4 inch thick. With a sharp knife, cut out eight 4-inch triangles from the dough, rerolling and cutting again if necessary. Transfer the dough triangles to the second lined baking sheet and prick the dough with a fork in a few spots on each piece. Brush with the egg wash and sprinkle with the sugar. Bake until light golden brown, 20 to 25 minutes.

○ For the filling, in a large sauté pan over high heat, combine the butter and sugars and cook until they start to caramelize. Turn the heat off and carefully add the apples, cinnamon stick, nutmeg, and salt. Now add the Calvados and turn the heat back on to medium-high. Carefully ignite the alcohol and let it flambé for a minute. Add the wine and flip the apples in the pan over the heat until the liquid is simmering and evaporates slightly and the apples are cooked but crisp, 1 to 2 minutes.

○ To serve, set a triangle of baked pastry on each plate. Spoon the sautéed apples and top with a couple of spoons of the baked streusel. Place the remaining 4 triangles on top. Serve immediately with whipped cream or ice cream, if desired.

Grilled PEACHES and APRICOTS with YOGURT, HONEY, and PISTACHIOS

If you are grilling ourdoors in the summer, leave the grill on for this quick dessert, which is inspred by Turkish-Mediterranean cuisine and very refreshing. This is just perfect when I really want something to end a meal but don't want it too sweet. To cook on the stove, sear the peaches and apricots in a hot cast-iron skillet.

SERVES 2 TO 4

2 peaches, halved and pitted

2 apricots, halved and pitted

1 tablespoon olive oil

1 to 2 tablespoons honey

4 ounces plain whole-milk, low-fat, or nonfat
 Greek yogurt

$1/4$ teaspoon orange blossom water

$1/4$ cup shelled pistachios, coarsely chopped,
 for garnish

○ Preheat a grill to high or heat a cast-iron grill pan over high heat on the stove.

○ Toss the peach and apricot halves with the olive oil, being sure to coat all sides. Set the fruit halves, cut side down, on the hot grill or pan. Grill until grill marks appear, 2 to 3 minutes. Remove from the heat and drizzle with the honey. Combine the yogurt and orange blossom water in a small bowl.

○ To serve, divide the yogurt mixture between bowls. Put the peach and apricot halves on top of the yogurt. Garnish with the chopped pistachios and serve.

RASPBERRIES with ROSE YOGURT

Raspberries and rose water are a match made in heaven. I have made many desserts with the combination of the fruit and the flower, and they seem to virtually just belong together. This is such an easy dessert and quite healthy, in fact. If I'm eating something heavier for dinner, such as roasted chicken and potatoes, I might want something light and fruity like this for dessert. This is also good for breakfast. A note on rose water: The various brands are different strengths. I usually start with a little bit, taste, and add more if necessary.

SERVES 4

1 pint fresh raspberries

1/8 to 1/4 teaspoon rose water

2 tablespoons honey

2 tablespoons freshly squeezed orange juice

8 ounces plain whole-milk Greek yogurt

○ In a bowl, combine half of the raspberries and all of the rose water, honey, and orange juice. Use a fork to mash lightly and set aside for a few minutes.

○ To serve, divide the raspberry–rose water sauce among 4 bowls. Divide the yogurt among the bowls. Top each serving with fresh raspberries over the yogurt.

Index

Acknowledgments

This book was made possible with the help and inspiration of the following people, places, and things: Women Chefs and Restaurateurs, because 20 years ago all of the chefs at the first WCR Gala inspired me for a lifetime. I have never forgotten those women who have worked so hard in this industry. And: SFAI, Zuni, Chez Panisse, the Edible Schoolyard, Sandra Bernhard, Laurie Anderson, Kate Bush, Muse, Serge Gainsbourg, Van Halen, Starchefs!, Les Dames d'Escoffier, Matt Accarrino, Sherry Yard, JP at Preferred Meats, Mitch at Aloha Fish, Dominique Crenn, Emily Luchetti, Nancy Oakes, Foo Fighters, Royce da 5'9", Bow Wow Wow, Pink, Sonic Youth, and the movie *Run Lola Run*. And thank you San Francisco, I have learned so much from the city where I lived for 25 years.

Frankie Frankeny for all of the amazing photography and being my best bud. And Chloe Harris Frankeny, both of you are so supportive, I love cooking and eating with you and the dachshund round up.

Wes Martin, who I have known since Rubicon and back when he was in the studio kitchen with Martha Stewart and who tested everything in this book with details galore.

Michael Psaltis, my agent, who actually totally gets me. Jenny Wapner, my editor, who has kicked some butt and made it happen. And Aaron Wehner at Ten Speed who has been a long time Citizen Cake/EF fan. Toni Tajima, art director at Ten Speed, who has put together the design and layout of this book.

Lexi Barry and Esther Paek, who I have rocked it out with on several occasions, and everyone who worked at Orson, the bakery, and Citizen Cake, because we have made some amazing food together over the last decade and a half.

Barbara Lynch and Gabrielle Hamilton, thank you! You have been so close to me over the last couple of years and have been there for me, cooked for me, and loved me. I have learned so much from you both. Kathleen Blake, thank you for your timing and virtually hearing me finish the book and for loving me.

Alton Brown, particularly for winking at me when I talked about the powers of xanthan gum, Judy Joo, Simon Majumdar, Iron Chef Michael Symon, for all the comments and judging NIC. Thank you to Steve Kroopnick, John Bravakas, Eytan Keller, Mary Donaldson, Les Thomas, and The Chairman for such an amazing TV experience. The production crew and culinary production crew (particulary for the fun dance party in Montauk, Long Island) from Triage Entertainment for the wild ride of Next Iron Chef 2011 and all my competitors: GZ, AG, AB, MC, MS, CH, RI, BeauMac, Spike.

I never felt more complete cooking and competing for something and having so much fun doing it!

Annika Kahn, my wise Jungshin Fitness trainer for coaching my body and core.

And Sean . . . for all my boxing moves.

Kate Bednarski for coaching my mind and Trace Cohen, who let me test and practice and for supporting me as only true friends do.

Cintra Wilson, who is wiser and more poetic than most of the world can handle. I adore your brilliance, you are the earth mother-f...ing rock star, simply gorgeous and piercingly hilarious.

Traci Des Jardins, who I always look up to.

Nancy Puglisi, I am excited to write the next chapter with you!

My family; my cousin, Hollie for calling me on game day, my mom, John, my dad, Pat, Mary, Steve, Ryan, and Jason for all of our great times together around the table, and of course Hudson and Hendrix, who are my favorite sous chefs!

Published in the United States by Ten Speed Press,

an imprint of the Crown Publishing Group,

a division of Random House, Inc., New York.

www.crownpublishing.com

www.tenspeed.com

Ten Speed Press and the Ten Speed Press colophon are registered trademarks of Random House, Inc.

Library of Congress Cataloging-in-Publicaion Data

Falkner, Elizabeth.

Cooking off the clock / Elizabeth Falkner.

p. cm.

1. Cooking. 2. Cookbooks. I. Title.

TX714.F3365 2012

641.5—dc23

2011041263

ISBN: 978-1-60774-030-8

eISBN: 978-1-60774-209-8

Printed in China

Cover and text design by Toni Tajima

10 9 8 7 6 5 4 3 2 1

First Edition